BRIGHT NOTES

MADAME BOVARY AND THREE TALES

BY

GUSTAVE FLAUBERT

Intelligent Education

INFLUENCE PUBLISHERS

Nashville, Tennessee

BRIGHT NOTES: Madame Bovary and Three Tales

www.BrightNotes.com

No part of this publication may be used or reproduced in any manner whatsoever without written permission, except in the case of brief quotations in critical articles and reviews. For permissions, contact Influence Publishers http://www.influencepublishers.com.

ISBN: 978-1-645421-78-8 (Paperback)
ISBN: 978-1-645421-79-5 (eBook)

Published in accordance with the U.S. Copyright Office Orphan Works and Mass Digitization report of the register of copyrights, June 2015.

Originally published by Monarch Press.
Arthur Rozen, 1965
2020 Edition published by Influence Publishers.

Interior design by Lapiz Digital Services. Cover Design by Thinkpen Designs.

Printed in the United States of America.

Library of Congress Cataloging-in-Publication Data forthcoming.
Names: Intelligent Education
Title: BRIGHT NOTES: Madame Bovary and Three Tales
Subject: STU004000 STUDY AIDS / Book Notes

CONTENTS

INTRODUCTION TO GUSTAVE FLAUBERT

NOTE TO THE READER

Madame Bovary may not be an easy book to like. If the student reading the novel for the first time finds it somehow cold or unsympathetic, puzzling or "monotonous," he will be in respectable company. Such has been the initial reaction of many intelligent readers, even though virtually all critics agree the book is a masterpiece of modern literature. The difficulties in reading the book in English cannot be attributed to a loss of "style" in translation. For, although style is the least translatable element of writing, and although the ultimate distinction of *Madame Bovary* is precisely its beauty of style, the above objections have frequently been raised against the French original.

In any discussion of the book, the possibility of such negative reactions had better be faced at once. They should be acknowledged even by those whose initial reaction is quite positive, those who are stirred to wonder and enthusiasm by Flaubert's supreme artistry and passion. The novel is a complicated and deeply ambiguous work, and the proper aim of its study is not so much to expel the reader's "mixed feelings," as to help him understand them. Hopefully, he will discover that *Madame Bovary* is one of those rare books whose fascination and value is in arousing the most inextricably mixed and poignantly contradictory emotions.

FLAUBERT'S LIFE: CHILDHOOD AND YOUTH

Gustave Flaubert was born on the twelfth of December 1821, in the Rouen hospital which his father administered. The Flauberts were a respected family in the city, though of relatively humble origins, and it was only through the talent and hard work of Dr. Flaubert that the family had achieved their solid middle-class position. Though too busy to give much time to his children, he was revered by them. Dr. Lariviere of *Madame Bovary*, the book's one truly admirable character, is obviously modeled on him.

During his early boyhood, Gustave's constant companion was his sister, Caroline. The family lived in an apartment adjoining the hospital, and frequently the two children climbed up to the window of the dissecting-room to stare at the peeled and dismembered cadavers. These experiences helped form an enduring fascination for the horrible, as reflected by the episodes of the clubfoot and Emma's death in *Madame Bovary*, and they contributed to Flaubert's recurrent revulsion against the physical side of life. The boy became an omnivorous reader of the standard French classics and the popular romantic fiction of the day. He organized a company of friends to perform plays of his own composition on his father's billiard table. These childhood works were filled with murders and corpses, moonlight and apparitions. He was adept at imitations, and one impersonation of an epileptic beggar (like the blind tramp of *Madame Bovary*) was so gruesomely vivid it had to be forbidden.

It was not personal experience alone that shaped his imagination. Gustave grew up during the height of the French

Romantic movement. The stirring days of the French Revolution and the Napoleonic Empire were now over, replaced by a colorless and repressive Bourbon monarchy, by the sordid money-hunger and drab commercialism of the middle-class, the bourgeoisie. A generation longing for vanished (and exaggerated) glory, whose imaginations had fed on Scott and Byron, Rousseau, Hugo, Dumas, and George Sand, turned to whatever was most remote from ordinary life, most extravagant and wild-even, if all else failed to relieve the boredom, suicide, the ultimate romantic gesture. Such was the fate, in fact, of two of Flaubert's Rouen schoolmates.

At school, Gustave soon discovered that while many of the boys seemed superficially like him, most were what he came to call "false romantics," mere followers of a fashion, who like Leon of *Madame Bovary* would soon lapse into complacent bourgeois. One close friend remained, the melancholy and sceptical Alfred Le Poittevin, who encouraged him to write his first lyrical and autobiographical works, *Memoirs of a Madman* (1838) and *November* (1843). Curiously, both works dealt with infatuations or affairs with married women: adultery was always fascinating to Flaubert.

In 1841, in obedience to his father's wishes, Flaubert enrolled as a law student in Paris. It was not a career he would have chosen himself, he whose motto was "Hatred of the bourgeoisie is the beginning of virtue." He found law school intolerably dull, and began writing a third book, *The Sentimental Education*, dealing with the growing up and gradual estrangement of two friends, one a true romantic, one a false. As a consequence of such extra-curricular activities, he failed his examinations. He resolved to try again, but in January 1844 an event occurred which changed his life. Flaubert was driving down a dark country road with his older brothers Achille, when they heard the sound of a wagon coming around a bend. Suddenly, as the separate lights of a nearby farmhouse, the approaching wagon, and Flaubert's own carriage, merged, he felt an uncanny sensation. A "golden incandescence" seemed to flare up within him in response to the outer light and grew brighter and brighter, bearing a dazzling and delightful tide of images, of "thousands" of memories and dreams from his past life. He passed out, to awake hours later exhausted and depressed. In the following weeks he had several similar attacks, which have been diagnosed only as an "atypical" form of epilepsy, and his frightened family decided-to his immense relief-that Gustave would be unable to continue law school. Thus, at the age of twenty-three Flaubert "retired" to the family villa at Croisset, a town on the Seine near Rouen, where he was to spend most of the remainder of his life.

LIFE AT CROISSET

It would be misleading, however, to think of Flaubert as a recluse to whom nothing ever happened. Even at Croisset there were tragedies: the death of his sister Caroline, his father, and his beloved Alfred Le Poittevin within the next four years. Even at Croisset there were friends: the young writer Maxime du Camp, the poet Louis Bouilhet, and later such correspondents as George Sand, Turgenev, and Maupassant. When his health improved, he spent a summer touring in Brittany and two years in the Near East with Maxime. In addition, whenever he could tear himself away from his work and his adored and anxious mother, there were brief excursions to Paris. During one of these trips in 1846 he began the only major love affair of his life.

Louise Colet was thirteen years older than Flaubert, separated from her husband, and mother of a little girl by Victor Cousin, the statesman and philosopher. She was a romantic poetess, of mediocre talent, though twice winner of the French Academy's poetry prize. The affair was intense and intermittent, dragged out by letters and reconciliations for almost ten years. The difficulty lay first in Flaubert's obstinate refusal to leave Croisset, his work and his mother, and settle in Paris: occasional passionate weekends were enough for him. Later, he grew disenchanted with Louise's character, her possessiveness, jealousy, violence, affectation, bad taste. She is thought to have partly inspired his portrait of Emma Bovary-even presenting him on one occasion a cigar-holder bearing the name motto, Amor nel cor, that is found on the signet ring Emma gives Rodolphe.

HIS EARLY WORK

But Flaubert's real life was his work, to which he gave a priestlike devotion, spending days to hammer out a perfect sentence, untempted by fashion or ambition for fame. Only once did a book come "easily" to him, his fourth work, *The Temptation of Saint Anthony*, an account of the devil's temptation of the third-century Christian hermit, filled with exotic imagery and esoteric lore. This was, in a way, Flaubert's favorite book, a kind of extravagant self-portrait of the "hermit" of Croisset, but when he read it to *Maxine du Camp* and Louis Bouilhet in 1849, his two friends criticized it mercilessly. It was, Bouilhet said, verbose, formless, imitative, and overly romantic. Flaubert should write, he said, a realistic story of everyday bourgeois life, something like Balzac.

BACKGROUND OF MADAME BOVARY

Some two years later, after Flaubert had returned from his tour of the Near East, Bouilhet reverted to their earlier conversation.

He began telling Flaubert about a certain Delamare, a former student of Dr. Flaubert's and health officer in a town near Rouen, who after the death of his first wife, a widow older than himself, had married the young daughter of a nearby farmer. Charming, convent-educated, young Madame Delamare soon grew to loathe her husband and country life, took lovers, sank into debt, and finally poisoned herself. Her husband, who had been blind to his wife's infidelities, was unable to live without her and killed himself too, leaving their little girl to his mother's care. This, said Bouilhet, is the story Flaubert should write, if he could discipline his style, and curb the romanticism which even he recognized as a "disease. . . ."

And so, after initial objections to the narrowness and vulgarity of the **theme**, Flaubert subdued himself to his masterpiece. Day after day he sat down in his study at Croisset for seven or more hours of the "sweet torment" of composition, searching for the "mot juste" (the one and only "right word"), crushing **metaphors** "like vermin," polishing his sentences and paragraphs. So deeply was he involved in his work that after writing the passages about Emma's suicide, he had the "taste of arsenic" in his mouth and actually vomited his dinner. When not writing he was reading medical books and journals or verifying scenes by visits to Rouen and the neighboring countryside. In April 1856, after almost five years work, *Madame Bovary* was finished.

THE BOOK'S EFFECT

The book first appeared, considerably expurgated, in installments in *Maxime du Camp's Revue de Paris*, and caused an immediate sensation. Its originality and beauty were recognized by discerning critics, while the **realism** and **satire** of its depiction of provincial life and of Emma's infidelities aroused wide-spread indignation Norman pharmacists, believing that Flaubert had used them as the model for Homais, thought of calling him out for a duel, and "the ladies" were scandalized by his slander of French female virtue. Finally, inspired by this furor and certain political motives, the government of Louis Napoleon prosecuted Flaubert for the "outrage of public morals and religion." But the trial, a milestone in the history of freedom of expression, ended with the Court voting for complete acquittal.

LATER WORKS

After *Madame Bovary*, giving vent to his long repressed exoticism, Flaubert turned to ancient Carthage in *Salammbo* (1862), a lush "prose opera" dealing with a revolt of mercenaries during the boyhood of Hannibal. Seven years later he published a final version of *Sentimental Education*, and in 1872 a third version of *The Temptation of Saint Anthony*. The first had grown from a study of true and false romanticism to a panoramic portrait of French society between 1840 and 1851, while the *Temptation* had been radically revised and cut. In 1874, after the unsuccessful production of his one play, *The Candidate*, Flaubert began his last novel, Bouvard and Pecuchet, a satirical account of two retired clerks who set about, in a succession of enthusiasms, to master the whole of 19th century knowledge. This work was to culminate in a project which had interested Flaubert from his youth, a *Dictionary of Accepted Ideas*, a compilation of all the most banal and half-baked notions of the time. *The Three Tales* was published in 1877, at the end of a vacation Flaubert had allowed himself from the anguish and monotony of his labors on Bouvard and Pecuchet. The latter book was never completed and was published posthumously in 1881.

FLAUBERT'S LATER LIFE

Flaubert's life, after *Madame Bovary*, was not marked by any momentous change, though perhaps superficially more varied than in earlier years. The novel had put him at the head of the French realists, widened his acquaintanceship and correspondence, and he now gave more time to the Paris literary world. Though his later years were darkened by the death of his mother and Louis Bouilhet, his own poor health, the financial difficulties of his beloved niece, Caroline, and gloomier forebodings of the destiny of art and civilization, in private life he remained a warm-hearted and companionable man. With all his literary misanthropy, he had a talent for friendship and a largeness of soul which is reflected not only in the way he received Bouilhet's criticism of *The Temptation of Saint Anthony* but in his later service as friend and teacher of Guy de Maupassant. It was the latter who thus melodramatically described Flaubert's death on May 8, 1880: "Finally one day he fell, stricken, against the foot of his work-table, killed by Her, by Literature; killed as are all great passionate souls by the passion that fires them." A fitting and somewhat ironic description for the death of the creator of Emma Bovary.

MADAME BOVARY IN LITERATURE

Any consideration of *Madame Bovary* should begin with some indication of its general place in literature. The book has had the greatest influence not only on French, but European, Russian and American novels of the modern era. Henry James, Zola, Conrad, Proust, Joyce, Virginia Woolf - to name only a few - are all indebted to Flaubert, and it may be said that wherever the novel has been conceived as "Art" - as distinct from mere entertainment, document, or self-display - *Madame Bovary* has been at least an indirect inspiration.

THE BOOK'S INNOVATIONS

Three kinds of innovating influence may be singled out: *Madame Bovary* raised the stature of the novel, modified novel technique, and helped give a new direction to romanticism.

First, Flaubert's work established the novel as a major art form, an objective showing-forth of life through the medium of highly-wrought, "architecturally" ordered language, uncircumscribed by the author's personal viewpoint or the rule of strict, straightforward narrative development. Before him, the novel's reality had been diminished by continual intrusions of the author's comments and analyses, its freedom restricted by the need to follow a chronological progression of events, its literary stature limited by the fact that no one had tried to give it formal and stylistic perfection rivaling poetry. By changing these conditions, Flaubert raised the novel to the major literary form of our era.

The most famous of Flaubert's technical innovations have been suggested above: the doctrine of le mot juste or "the right word" (with its corollary of the all-importance of the right prose rhythm) and the doctrine of the novel's "impersonality" or the writer's "impassivity." Flaubert said that the writer should be like God in his work, "everywhere present, but nowhere visible." Other innovations, however, are equally important. First of all, there is his reliance on the "symbolic" method of construction, rather than straightforward narration. True, there is a fairly regular chronological progression in *Madame Bovary*, but the novel really hangs together through a series of symbols or symbolic episodes. Consider, for instance, the role played by the **theme** of "travel" in Emma's life: her dreams of exotic journeys matched against her trips on the "Hirondelle" (the Yonville coach), her horseback ride with Rodolphe, her cab ride with Leon. In addition, the straight-line chronological development is undercut by three other characteristic devices: the revery, the repetition, and the "double action." Continually, we find Emma returning in flashbacks or reveries to memories of the convent or her father's farm; over and over, as in her periodic spells of religious enthusiasm, we find her reverting to an earlier mood or character; again and again, as in the first conversation of Leon and Emma, the country fair scene, the amputation of the clubfoot's leg, we find two opposed actions being carried on simultaneously. Through these devices, and the use of symbols, the novel acquires a quality of "architectural" or must musical symmetry (Flaubert called *Madame Bovary* a "sonata") and forsakes the linear progression of the tale: ". . . This happened, then this happened, then this. . . ."

Finally, there is Flaubert's role as a transformer of romanticism. Through his outward criticism and inward allegiance to romanticism in *Madame Bovary*, he helped give the movement a new vitality, and most major modern writers still work in a tradition recognizably "romantic." As critic, he revealed in Emma Bovary the weaknesses and internal contradictions of the sentimental and "literary" romantic. He clearly defined, moreover, romanticism's worst external enemies: the vulgar materialism of a Homais, Bournisien, Lheureux the sheer bourgeois cloddishness of a Charles Bovary. But above all, he accommodated romanticism to the two intellectual movements which most opposed it: science and "classicism". His writing had an objectivity, precision, respect for fact, researched thoroughness, which allied it to the scientific spirit. It had a polish and order, a clarity and self-restraint, a concern for the universal or the type, which affiliated it to 17th century French classicism.

PROBLEMS OF MADAME BOVARY

Returning to the problem raised at the beginning of this introduction, the possibility of the student's "mixed feelings" upon reading *Madame Bovary*, we find that such feelings are likely to stem from four things: Flaubert's treatment of his characters, particularly Emma and Charles Bovary; his ambiguous attitude toward romanticism and the bourgeoisie; a sense of his general "nihilism," or revulsion against life; and a certain "monotony" or uniformity in the book.

FLAUBERT'S TREATMENT OF CHARACTER

Since Flaubert's treatment of his heroine and her husband is so problematical, it is a subject well-suited for an examination or a student paper. Therefore, a fuller discussion will be reserved for the section on Essay Questions and Answers. We can say here, however, that although Emma clearly embodies some of the most shallow and contemptible features of sentimental romanticism, that although Flaubert almost sadistically hounds her to ruin and horrible death, sometimes even forsaking his vaunted "impassivity" to show his scorn for her, she nevertheless remains a character for whom he cannot help but feel sympathy. To the inevitable question, "Who is Madame Bovary?" Flaubert customarily replied, "Madame Bovary, c'est moi." ("I am Madame Bovary.") Flaubert's great, consistent **themes** are temptation and martyrdom, and in Emma Bovary he sees not only a person succumbing to his own temptations and potential weaknesses, but one who, through the discrepancy between her vision and reality, through the implacable stupidity of the world, suffers a genuine "martyrdom." With Charles, too, we find the same bewildering and typical alternation between indignation and pity, contempt and affection.

FLAUBERT'S VIEW OF ROMANTICISM

Emma Bovary was both bourgeois and romantic, and so was Flaubert. This is always an uneasy combination, though we may exclude from Flaubert's makeup certain of the romantic traits which dominated Emma. Romanticism began as a reaction against an artificial and limited view of life, the 18th century tendency to regard man, society and the natural world as kinds of inalterable "machines," to rigidly separate man from nature, to exalt reason as man's primary and distinguishing faculty, to accept the status quo as something divinely ordained and immutable. Romanticism protested, in the name of truth, that the universe was not a machine, that nature and man were intimately connected, that feeling and imagination were as important to humanity as reason, and that society and the individual had limitless possibilities of growth and change. But Emma's romanticism, like that of many others, has nothing to do with a search for truth, rather it makes it ultimately impossible for her to recognize reality or goodness, to have any genuine, unaffected feelings or tastes. It may be said that Flaubert, recognizing romanticism's power of enhancing the meaning of life, of granting heroic possibilities to the individual imagination, wished to restore it to the truth. What the romantic imagination can do at its best may be seen in practically every description and revery in *Madame Bovary*, those astonishing and poetic passages which so strangely oppose and modify their banal environment. In *Madame Bovary*, then, we have a criticism of romanticism made in the name of romanticism, and partly carried out by romantic means.

FLAUBERT'S VIEW OF THE BOURGEOISIE

There can be no simple interpretation of Flaubert's attitudes to the bourgeoisie, either. He who signed letters "Gustavus Flaubertus Bourgeoisphobus" ("Bourgeois-hater") came from a solid middle-class family and lived (mostly) in a solid middle-class way. Romanticism and scientific rationalism, the two forces which had shaped his imagination, were basically middle-class creations, and he remained true to many middle-class values: self-reliance, self-discipline, hard work, family feeling, etc. With all the ire poured down upon Homais, the embodiment of bourgeois self-interest, materialism and stupidity, there is a grudging respect for some of the bourgeois virtues of Charles, old Rouault, and even Emma herself. The characters who arouse Flaubert's deepest scorn, the idlers, dilettantes, quacks, incompetents, those whose labor is purely self-interested or useless, are condemned so severely because they fail to measure up to the highest bourgeois standard of useful, competent and dedicated labor. Thus, Charles falls from grace when, in operating on the clubfoot, he adventures outside of true professionalism; while, at Emma's death, as if to redress the imminent triumph of the quacks and scoundrels (Homais, Bournisien, Lheureux), Flaubert intrudes the description of Dr. Lariviere, the model of a middle-class professional.

FLAUBERT'S "NIHILISM"

Seriously interpreted, then, both romantic and middle-class values constitute ideals to which the world seldom conforms.

A serious bourgeois romantic like Flaubert, especially one endowed with an early and instinctive horror of life (so he claimed), would find many occasions for nihilism and spleen. Even the central values of his heritage, Labor and Vision, might become ambiguous.

Dedicated labor is necessary; it is what gives dignity to the life of a Dr. Lariviere, a Catherine Ledoux (the old peasant woman at the fair). But in the end, the world being so stupid and ungrateful, what good is it? Vision means, first, seeing the world as it is, for the truth should be useful and morally bracing, however bad. But what if, stripping the world of illusion, one comes to conclude the world itself is illusion? Vision means, second, Flaubert's "mystic" glimpses of an ideal state "so superior to life that compared to its glory would be nothing, and happiness vain." But these moments, when Flaubert looked at the natural world or into his own past and suddenly transcended the abyss between self and non-self, past and present, might end in a sense of self-dissolution or profound depression. What, then, if those things which most justified consciousness-vision, love-tended to end in the very disintegration of consciousness?

These are difficult questions to answer, and sometimes we may even feel that Flaubert punishes Emma so terribly not just because she was a "false romantic," but because she dared to believe in happiness. Nevertheless, however powerful was the strain of nihilism or life-hatred in Flaubert, he committed himself to the highest combined form of Labor and Vision: Art. Whatever the abysses of blackness and nothingness in *Madame Bovary,* the reader may feel that the supreme artistry of every page represents a sufficient affirmation by the author at least.

THE TONE OF MADAME BOVARY

Finally, there is the question of the "monotony" of *Madame Bovary* a consequence of Flaubert's steadfast effort to achieve the "style of truth" through an unremitting struggle against imprecision, the drag of existing **conventions** of fiction, and powerful tendencies of his own imagination. Flaubert conceived of normal bourgeois life, such as the Bovary's, as basically an even and directionless flow, and to render these qualities truly every effort had to be made to preserve the "factual equality" of events. That is, even though a novel must have its peaks of tension and meaning, its overall design, the realistic or "scientific" writer would try-insofar as possible-to seem not to prefer one event, one fact, over another. The result would be a narrative composed of a series of independent and equally values pictures, with a certain levelness of tone. This quality is enhanced by the regularity and repetitiousness of the major phases in Emma's life, and by the general consistency of tone prescribed by the doctrine of "impassivity" or "impersonality." The same kinds of events occur over and over, and are allowed to speak for themselves without the usual coloration of pity, indignation, judgement, etc. A basic tenet of Flaubert's are is respect for the surface particularity of events or facts; they are not to be violated by opinion or analysis, or the usual kind of identification with the **protagonist**. The presence of the writer is only felt through his careful selection of detail and precision of language. Thus, the reader will understand that the appearance of a "great smooth line," a bare unbroken "wall," is exactly the effect Flaubert wished to achieve.

MADAME BOVARY

PART 1

. . . .

CHAPTER ONE

The story begins in a boy's school in Rouen, a city in northern France, around 1830. The narrator, who had been one of the students, recalls the sensation created by the introduction of Charles Bovary into his classroom. A clumsy, overgrown country boy of fifteen, dressed in ill-fitting clothing, Bovary is particularly encumbered by his new, going-to-school cap, described as a weird composite of the "bearskin, lancer's cap, bowler, nightcap, and otterskin." After fumbling with this article and having it knocked to the floor by a classmate, Charles is asked for his name. His first words are unintelligible, but then, thoroughly confused, he shouts at the top of his voice "Charbovari!" to be answered by the mimicking hoots and laughter of his classmates. Placed in the dunce's seat, he diligently and silently sets to work on the task assigned by his teacher: twenty repetitions of the phrase ridiculous sum: "I am ridiculous."

Comment

The action of *Madame Bovary* takes place between 1830 and 1848, during the reign of Louis Philippe, a period known for its devotion to money-making and doctrines of economic and technological "progress," its indifference to genuine spiritual values, taste and art. Charles' cap, in its vulgarity, pretentiousness, incongruous mixture of styles and materials, essential ugliness, stands as a symbol of the age.

The story is begun by a narrator, identified only as a former classmate of Charles, who disappears from the novel by the middle of the chapter. His presence gives authority and immediacy to the opening events. Thereafter, however, he could only diminish the objectivity of the narration, while his intimate knowledge of all characters and events would be incredible to the reader. The story focuses initially on Charles, rather than Emma, the principal character. Charles must be delineated fully because he is the primary element in Emma's dissatisfaction and rebellion. Moreover, since the final chapters also deal exclusively with Charles, this treatment lends a certain symmetry to the novel.

Charles' parents are described in a flashback. His father, a former army doctor, is a conceited wastrel, who, after running through most of his wife's money, has retired to a small farm, giving himself up to drink and debauchery, and turning, in the process, his wife's idolatrous love to sullen hatred. Charles, the child of this union, is spoiled by his mother, neglected by his father. The boy becomes the focus of his mother's frustration and ambition: she teaches him to read, sees that he receives the rudiments of Latin from the village priest, dreams of his becoming rich and famous. After a sketchy education-what he chiefly cares about is helping on the farm, rambling in the fields-Charles is sent to school in Rouen. The narrator remembers him as good-natured, timid, solitary, conscientious enough to keep in the middle of his class, thoroughly mediocre.

Comment

Some of Charles' basic traits are formed early in life by his parents, particularly his timorousness and general passivity. About all, he is used to being dominated by a woman, to shaping his life to please a woman. He completely lacks ambition or strong personal motivation. Other qualities, however, seem innate and more positive: about all the good-natured simplicity which is unaffected by parental mistreatment and will survive the worst of future blows.

After his third year in school, Charles enrolled in the medical college at Rouen. He is stunned by the difficulty of the work and, after a period of dutiful, uncomprehending drudgery, stops attending lectures. He begins to spend his time in cheap cafes, reveling in his idleness, playing dominoes by the hour, and otherwise being initiated into the "forbidden pleasures." He fails his examinations, discloses his recent life to his mother, and is sent back for another try. This time he succeeds. His mother finds a medical practice for him in Tostes, a small town, and-to go with it-a wife, one Madame Dubuc. A widow, forty-five years old, "ugly, thin as a lath, with as many pimples as the spring has buds." Madame Dubuc has the attraction of a small income. Charles finds himself the servant of a capricious, hypochondriacal old woman who reads his mail, spies on his consultations, and complains perpetually of his coldness and neglect.

Comment

Charles' degree is not equivalent to the American MD; he is not qualified as a physician, but as a "health officer," a much less highly-trained practitioner intended for general rural needs. At the end of Chapter One we find Charles, after an interval of the most modest dissipation and rebellion, once again firmly under female domination.

CHAPTER TWO

Late one night a messenger wakens Charles Bovary requesting him to go immediately to a farm called Les Bertaux to set a broken leg. Since the distance from Tostes to Les Bertaux is eighteen miles, and since it is a dark, rainy winter night and "Bovary's bride is afraid of accidents," Charles waits until about four in the morning to start out. As he rides along through the flat somber countryside in the first light, still half-asleep, vivid images of his past and present life combine strangely in his mind. At Vassonville a small boy sent as a guide meets Charles and engages him in conversation as he leads the way. From this child Charles learns that M. Rouault is a fairly well-to-do farmer; that he had broken his leg returning from a Twelfth Night carousal; and that he is a widower whose daughter, the "young lady," keeps house for him.

Comment

The arrival of a messenger at night, Charles' journey at dawn, his half-conscious review of his life, are traditional signs in literature that the "hero is embarking on an adventure and that a fateful event is about to occur. However, the romantic possibilities of these scenes are greatly qualified by the realistic, rather comic details with which we are supplied. For instance, the maid chatting from her window with the messenger; the middle-aged wife modestly turning to the wall when the messenger enters; the incongruous medley of images in Charles' imagination as he rides to the farm: "A warm smell of poultices mingled in his consciousness with the sharp tang of the dew, the sound of iron rings running along the curtain rods over the beds . . . with his wife sleeping." We shall see throughout *Madame Bovary* that the scrupulous objectivity of the author's view always keeps the stone very down to earth.

Les Bertaux proves to be a solid, busy, well-kept place and its owner an energetic, plump man of fifty. To his relief Charles finds that M. Rouault's fracture is a simple one, easily set. While Rouault's daughter, Mademoiselle Emma, is helping to sew bandages and later when she is giving him a snack in the kitchen, Charles notices how pretty she is. He is especially struck by the whiteness of her nails and by various touches of elegance in her hairstyle and dress. M. Rouault's leg mends quickly and the doctor is esteemed "first class." Charles finds that he likes visiting Les Bertaux and goes much more often than necessary, without knowing exactly why. His wife, however, discovering that old Rouault has a clever, convent-educated daughter immediately guesses why Charles always looks so happy when he sets out for the farm. "Instinctively" she hates Emma. She harangues Charles about the "hussy" and finally makes him swear on the prayer-book that he will stop visiting Les Bertaux. This prohibition only serves to strengthen Charles' love for Emma and to make him more aware, by contrast, of the widow's plainness and ill-temper.

Comment

Our first introduction to Emma gives us valuable clues to her character and the refined image she wishes to present to the world. Even on the farm she dresses in flounces and carries a parasol. In her first conversation with Charles she reveals how boring she finds life in the country. Her strangeness, delicacy, and beauty, the attentions she pays him and the respect he has received from M. Rouault combine to excite in Charles a sense of his worth, and, for the first time, a desire for something prompted only by his own feelings. Until this time he has never been self-motivated.

About two months later all the widow Dubuc's investments are embezzled. An investigation shows that the lady was never really worth as much as the Bovarys had assumed. M. Bovary is furious and accuses his wife of "ruining their son by hooking him up to an old harridan whose harness was no better than her hide." Within a few days of this uproar, the unfortunate widow has a stroke and dies. Charles feels quite sad. "She had loved him, after all."

CHAPTER THREE

M. Rouault visits Charles to pay him and to offer his sympathies. He had mourned for his own wife deeply and cannot realize that in Charles' case grief is mixed with a large portion of relief. Free now to does as he wishes, Charles responds gladly to Rouault's invitation to visit Les Bertaux. One hot summer afternoon Charles finds himself alone with Emma at the farmhouse. At first they are rather shy, but soon, speaking about their schooldays, they grow more at ease. Emma shows Charles various girlish souvenirs, speaks of her mother, the servant problem, her desire to live in town, her present boredom ... Charles is fascinated. That night he is sleepless thinking of her and resolves to ask for her hand.

Comment

Here Charles' feeling for Emma crystallizes. His love is abetted by his new-found independence, old Rouault's friendliness, and the richness of the season. Close-ups of Emma endow her with the charm of a discreet sensuality. We see her bare shoulders covered with little drops of perspiration as she sews by the window, her head thrown back as she drinks a liqueur, "the tip of her tongue between her fine teeth licking, drop by drop, the bottom of the glass." We hear her voice, now clear, now merry, now languorous, as she talks of her past and present life.

Old Rouault quickly sizes up the situation and is ready to let Emma go if Charles wants her. She is little use to him, being "too clever for farming." He considers Charles "rather a wisp of a man" but dependable and unlikely to demand a large dowry-convenient since Rouault is too comfort-loving to be a really good farmer and has been losing money steadily. After much procrastination, Charles finally gets up courage to speak to the old man. Rouault cuts short Charles' stammering with immediate assent, and volunteers to relay the proposal to his daughter. Emma, agrees, and the wedding is planned for the next spring, since Charles' mourning period must be observed. Although, typically, Emma would have preferred something more romantic - "torches at midnight" - preparations are made for a mammoth country-style wedding celebration, which will last three days and consist mainly of feasting and drinking.

Comment

Flaubert concentrates on the practical aspects of the wedding plans rather than on the engaged couple's feelings. This serves several purposes: we observe the characteristic bourgeois precedence of material matters above all else; we see that the conversations of Charles and Emma during this period revolve around such prosaic matters as deciding in which room to hold the wedding breakfast, and not with more intimate and personal questions; we surmise that Emma has little idea of her future husband and may have chosen to marry chiefly to escape from life on the farm. Finally, Flaubert wishes to keep Emma in the background-to have her seen only as Charles sees her-until after the wedding.

CHAPTER FOUR

The wedding of Charles and Emma is described in detail, Flaubert obviously relishing its picturesque and old-fashioned, lavish character. The guests arrive early in vehicles ranging from carriages to farm-carts, wearing various costumes, from dress-coats to smocks, according to their social status. All country types are there: prosperous farmers in starched shirts, their broad faces raw from close shaving; the wives in town dresses, with bonnet and shawl; the big girls nervous in their first long dresses; the little boys uncomfortable in their first boots. The wedding procession, led by a fiddler and trailed by frolicking children, winds through the fields from the church to the farm. A bounteous feast follows, climaxed by the masterpiece of the local pastry-cook: a three-tiered cake, representing a Greek temple surmounted by a castle surmounted by a green meadow with a Cupid on a chocolate swing.

Charles' father flirts with a peasant girl and drinks far into the night. His mother, who had not been consulted about the wedding, sulks and retires early. The bride and groom go to their room. Charles, who had responded feebly to the jests and innuendoes of the day, is spared-through his father-in-law's intervention-the customary horseplay outside the doors or windows of the bridal chamber. In the morning, Emma seems calm and unchanged, but Charles is obviously in a state of bliss, following his bride up and down, embracing her continually. After two days the couple leaves for Tostes. As old Rouault watches them drive away, he sadly remembers his own wedding, his early married life with the wife he loved.

Comment

In part, the wedding **episode** may be regarded as a tour de force of description. In its humorous **realism**, color and vitality it is a kind of animated "film version" of one of the Flemish paintings of peasant life. Though the wedding is a far cry from the romantic ceremony of Emma's dreams, it is a fair representation of the world she comes from and which, by her marriage to a doctor, she is technically rising above: the Rouault world of small farmers and peasants. It is clear that Flaubert, while noting vulgarity and meanness in this world, takes pleasure in its gusto and simplicity, its genuineness. Thus, as Emma commences her new life, begun in illusion and ending in deceit, it is not her thoughts we are made privy to, but old Rouault's memories of the wife he deeply and unaffectedly loved. The homely festivities, the old man's reflections, underscore Emma's pretentions and future disappointments.

CHAPTER FIVE

Emma's new home is small, tastelessly furnished, and rather dilapidated. In the bedroom the first Mme. Bovary's bridal bouquet is still on display. Emma stares as it, and while Charles carries it up to the attic, wonders what would happen to her own bouquet if she were to die. She spends the first few days of her married life redecorating the house. Charles is blissful. He adores his wife and everything about her, no matter how small, delights him. In the morning he rides off to see his patients "ruminating on his good fortune, like one who continues to savor the taste of the truffles while he digests his dinner." His wife is the first good thing that has ever happened to him and he dotes on her while she gently "pushes him away with a weary half-smile, as you do a child that hangs on to you." Emma had thought she was in love, but now considers that she must have been mistaken. Where are the feelings of sublime happiness, "passion," and "ecstasy" she had so often read about?

Comment

In this chapter Flaubert begins to shift the point of view toward Emma's consciousness. For the first time her thoughts are revealed to us. We see that she is already becoming disillusioned with Charles, whose somewhat gross and bovine contentment is perfectly suggested by the image of the man who keeps savoring the meal he has just eaten. Although the steps of this process are not stated explicitly, it is clear that the shabbiness of her house and the dullness of environment it reflects, plus the clumsy fatuousness of Charles' love-making, are among the sources of her disappointment.

CHAPTER SIX

Paul et Virginie, a popular romance depicting tender innocence and ill-fated adolescent love, had marked Emma's imagination at an early age. At thirteen she was sent to school at a convent. At first the girl was completely absorbed in the atmosphere and duties of piety, but her enthusiasm was emotional rather than spiritual: "it was necessary for her to derive a sort of personal profit from things, she rejected as useless whatever did not minister to her heart's immediate fulfillment." It was the incense, the ceremonies, the erotic **metaphors** of Christian love that excited her. When she was sixteen she plunged into the moonlit world of the romantic novels that were smuggled into the convent. In addition to Sir Walter Scott's castles and cavaliers, the lives of famous and martyred women, sentimental songs, the secret souvenirs given to her schoolmates by aristocratic admirers, portraits of coy languishing ladies, exotic scenes, all thrilled her.

Comment

The era of *Madame Bovary* marked the height of popular romanticism and its decadence, a betrayal of what Flaubert considered true romantic ideals. Blood, melancholy, and exoticism were the mode, and to some extent Emma is the victim of this rage. Gilded fantasies of love and adventure play a part in most young girl's lives, but Emma is uncommonly addicted to them and never emerges from these dreams to a mature poetic sensibility. By nature she is neither artistic nor warm-hearted. Unlike her wealthy schoolmates at the convent, she can find nothing in her simple background to match the glamor she covets; the refinements of her education can only serve to make her a misfit.

Her mother's death provided Emma with an occasion to experience the suffering she believed to be the ideal state of sensitive souls. For a few days she cried a great deal and in letters home expressed such sad and morbid ideas her father thought she must be sick. She luxuriated in tearfully lovely images and tragic postures until, despite her best efforts, she grew tired of this role. Almost simultaneously she became discontented with the narrow convent life, and her piety decreased with her growing resentment of school discipline. When she left the convent the nuns were not sorry to see her go. Back at the farm, Emma at first enjoyed managing the servants, but soon wearied of the country, regarding herself as completely knowing and disillusioned. However, the presence of Charles re-awakened her old longings and she had believed herself "possessed of that wonderful passion which hitherto had hovered above her like a great bird of rosy plumage." Now she awakes to the uneventful reality of her married life.

Comment

Emma's grief for her mother is described with **irony** because it is as short-lived and unreal as her religious phase and her love for Charles. Genuine feeling has been twisted in her. Her ideas of happiness and glory, formed by sentimental fictions, are essentially illusionary and she is bound to be frustrated by her husband's stolidity and the humble circumstances of their life.

CHAPTER SEVEN

Sometimes, however, the very disappointments of life with Charles induce delightful reveries which reflect a glow upon Emma's "honeymoon," making it seem the "finest time of her life." She sees herself ascending romantic mountains in a carriage with blue-silk blinds, hearing the tinkling of goat-bells and the rush of waterfalls; visualizes herself standing on the terrace of a villa, hand in hand with her husband, breathing the scent of lemon trees and gazing up at the stars.

Comment

The passage describing Emma's daydreams reveals much about the nature of her character and Flaubert's technique. We see, first of all, how she feels that happiness must be "legitimized" by romantic circumstance. She cannot believe in the reality of happiness without a glamorous background. We note, too, the relative precision of the bookish images of exotic landscapes compared to the vagueness of her picture of the husband sharing this felicity. He is little more than a window-dummy in black velvet coat and ruffled shirt. One should also recognize the subtle control of tone in this passage: how it shifts with the sentence "It seemed to her that certain parts of the world must produce happiness..." from nostalgic sweetness to melancholy yearning.

Emma realizes that she can never communicate her feelings to Charles. He is completely unimaginative and uninformed on all subjects that lend romantic interest to a man. His conversation is "as flat as a street pavement"; he cannot fence or shoot a pistol or introduce her into the mysteries of passion. But Charles is entirely happy, luxuriating in his good fortune and blind to her unrest. The only note of conflict he recognizes arises on the occasions of his mother's visits, the old woman resenting Emma's style of life and her engrossment of Charles' affection, the young woman irritated by her mother-in-law's interferences. Emma tries to make herself in love by reciting poetry in the garden, singing melancholy songs, but this has no effect on Charles' feelings or her own. Charles' passion, she feels, is becoming more routine, a kind of "habit."

Comment

A climactic **episode** in the record of Emma's disenchantment is a brief scene in a field outside Tostes near a derelict summerhouse. The "knife-edged" leaves of rushes in a ditch, the wallflowers and nettles in the field, the shutters of the summerhouse rotting away behind rusty bars, suggest Emma's desolation and despair. Her thoughts revolve aimlessly, at first, like her little dog that circles around the edge of the field, yapping at butterflies, then comes to a focus as she digs the point of parasol into the ground, crying "O God, O God, why did I marry?" This passage parallels the earlier revery - it is the reality which answers to her dreams - and shows again how Flaubert makes use of objective images of landscape and actions to convey the quality and development of a mood.

Emma thinks wistfully of the life she might have had with a different man. She imagines the glamorous life of her schoolmates and even regrets the lost excitement of prize days at the convent. Sometimes, after an afternoon of such meditation in the field, a wind springs up from the sea. Emma shivers, walks back through the straight avenue of rustling trees, feeling a touch of fear as she glances at the black trunks standing against the red sky. This is the first suggestion of the tragic destiny to which her dissatisfaction will inexorably lead her. The chapter concludes with the Bovarys receiving an invitation to a ball given by the local magnate, the Marquis d'Andervilliers, in gratitude for a cure accomplished by Charles.

CHAPTER EIGHT

The Bovarys arrive at La Vaubyessard, the estate of Marquis d'Andervilliers at night. Entering, Emma sees the dim portraits of the Marquis' ancestors in their gilt frames. Within, all is light and perfume: the flames of the chandeliers reflecting off the cut glass and silver dish-covers, the bouquet of flowers mingling with the odor of rich food. At dinner, Emma notices especially the Marquis' father-in-law, a red-eyed, drooling, senile old man, said to have once been the lover of Marie Antoinette. The quadrille begins and, in the intervals between dances, Emma overhears conversations about trips to Italy and triumphs on the race-course and witnesses a young lady passing a love letter under cover of a dropped fan. She is enraptured by the music, the novelty and richness of her surroundings, the beautiful costumes of the ladies, the elegance of the gentlemen. Her past life seems unreal.

Comment

To build up the lush, hot-house atmosphere of the chateau, Flaubert uses series of related images: the flowers on the table and in the ladies' hair, their perfume mingling with pomade and scent, their colors with the whiteness of table-linen, the men's dress-shirts, the women's bare shoulders, or with the scarlet of lobster claws, the turbans of the matrons, the red coats of Andervilliers' pictured ancestors, or with the gold of jewelry, gilt frames, scent bottles.

All the glamor and exoticism culminates, for Emma, in a small group of gentlemen of particularly elegant appearance: their clothes more exquisitely tailored, their hair and handkerchiefs more delicately scented, their skin of a special clear whiteness, "the complexion of wealth." The old among them have a youthful air, the young seem mature; all have a certain aura of nonchalance and subtle brutality, fostered by ease and easy conquests, the mastery of thoroughbred horses and easy women. Emma feels the glamor of this type; their qualities merge into her image of the ideal man-ultimately to be realized by Rodolphe, her first lover. She cannot see their limitations: the vanity and dissipation to which the repulsive old Duc de Laverdiere, the former lover of a queen, stands as monument.

After a supper as lavish as the dinner, the dancing resumes. A Viscount persuades Emma to try a waltz, a dance just coming into popularity and one unfamiliar to her. The two whirl over the dance-floor, their legs intertwining, until Emma almost swoons with the motion and excitement. The party breaks up. Charles, who had been forbidden to dance by his wife, falls asleep immediately, while Emma sits up until dawn, trying to prolong the rapture of the evening. In the morning, she is conducted through the estate, feeding the swans, visiting the greenhouse, orangery, and stables. As the Bovarys ride off in their little trap, they are passed by a troop of laughing gentlemen on horseback. Later, Charles finds a cigar case one of them has dropped. Back home, in an irritable mood, Emma dismisses the servant for failing to get dinner on time, is furious when Charles becomes sick attempting to smoke one of the cigars. In the days that follow, her memory of the ball fades, but she is conscious that her life has changed.

Comment

Flaubert remarks of Emma: "The visit to La Vaubyessard had made a gap in her life..." This is her first exposure to the actuality of a privileged existence; the first and fatal confirmation of her dreams. Now Charles, who cannot even smoke a cigar properly, and Tostes, with its shabbiness and boredom, are confronted with the memory of "real" glamor and excitement, not just images drawn from books. The **episode**, too, forms a brilliant contrast to the scenes at Emma's wedding. The one festivity is completely opposed to the other in terms of the type of guests present, manners, diversions, and physical surroundings.

CHAPTER NINE

The cigar-case, which keeps hidden, evokes wonderful memories and dreams, and Emma tries desperately to keep in touch with the sophisticated world. She buys a guide to Paris, subscribes to fashion and society papers, studies "descriptions of furniture" in novels of high life. The world of ambassadors, duchesses and artists represents for her the whole of humanity while her own ordinary environment strikes her as a freak. Emma tries to make a lady's maid of her little serving girl, buys ribbons, frills, perfumes and fashionable ornaments, calls ordinary dishes by extraordinary names and leads a completely idle life.

To Charles, who works hard all day, poking his arm into damp beds, letting blood, examining basins, tucking in dirty sheets, Emma's little refinements are a mystery and a pleasure, a "kind of gold dust." By being modest and upright and by sticking to simple remedies, Charles has established a good reputation around Tostes. He subscribes to a medical journal but falls asleep over it after dinner. Why, Emma wonders, couldn't she at least have married a silent but brilliant scholar? Charles is becoming repugnant to her. She despises his coarse manners but he mistakes her irritable concern for affection. Always Emma is waiting, waiting for something to happen that will suddenly change her life. October rolls round again but, to her great disappointment, there is no ball this year.

Comment

Incited by memories of the ball, Emma allows herself to withdraw more and more into dreams. Since she confounds "gilded sensuality with heart's delight, elegance of manner with delicacy of feeling," she thinks pretty objects may provide the proper atmosphere for the delicate plant of love. But the pedestrian real world, represented by Charles, cannot be kept at bay for long. The groom in wooden shoes will clump down the passage every morning and Charles, getting fat and gulping his soup, must be faced every evening.

As the days pass, hope fails and Emma abandons herself to misery. She gives up reading, playing the piano, drawing and, much to her mother-in-law's surprise, ceases to bother with the house or her appearance. The long, cold winter exactly matches her dark, lifeless mood. Every day is like the next. Once in a while, a gypsy passes by with a barrel organ that plays popular waltzes while tiny figures of peasants, monkeys and gentlefolk dance in a miniature drawing room. "Her thoughts leapt with the music."

Emma becomes capricious, unpredictable. She orders food, then eats nothing; refuses to go outdoors, then feels stifled, scolds the maid, then gives her presents. When her father comes to visit she finds his chatter about farming nerve-wracking. She no longer bothers to hide her negative feelings and expresses unconventional opinions that astonish her husband. She alternates between excitement and torpor, grows pale, thin coughs, has palpitations of the heart. It seems that there must be something about the air of Tostes that is injuring her and so, hard as it is for Charles to give up his good practice, he plans to move to Yonville l'Abbaye, near Rouen. One day as Emma is packing, she comes upon her withered wedding bouquet. She tosses it into the fire, "the shriveled paper petals hovered like black butterflies at the back of the fireplace and finally vanished up the chimney." When they leave Tostes in March, Madame Bovary is pregnant.

Comment

Flaubert describes with great psychological perception what today we would call neurotic "neurasthenia," a condition of general physical debility caused by emotional problems. Lacking an inner foundation, Emma values things only as they reflect upon her the glory of an imagined world. Why play the piano if one will never play at a concert with "murmurs of ecstasy wafting all about?" If Emma cannot make herself happy, she can make herself completely miserable and even ill. Alienated from the life around her, she turns the whole world into an echo of her boredom and bitterness.

Indirectly, Flaubert emphasizes the absurdity of her ideals by comparing Emma to the pathetic figure of the Tostes hairdresser who longs for a big shop in Rouen, and by developing the image of the barrel-grinder's entertainment, a grotesque **parody** of the ball at La Vaubyessard. The burning of her wedding bouquet provides an obvious symbol of Emma's now complete renunciations of her marriage.

MADAME BOVARY

. . . .

CHAPTER ONE

Flaubert leads the reader on an imaginary tour of Yonville, the sleepy backward little town which is to be the Bovarys' new home. Leaving the highroad, the traveler passes through an outer zone of ramshackle outhouses, walled yards and low, thatched cottages. In the center of town are the church, dilapidated and poorly furnished; the market place; the Town Hall, built like a miniature "Greek temple"; the pharmacy of Monsieur Homais with its red and green apothecary jars and placards advertising various medications; and the old inn, the "Golden Lion." There is nothing else to see except the cemetery at the farther end of town, where, in an empty patch of ground, the grave-digger grows potatoes-thus, as the village cure says, in a twofold sense "living on the dead."

Comment

Flaubert remarks that nothing has altered in Yonville since *Madame Bovary's* day. Among other things unchanged, he notes "the chemist's foetuses," which, "like bundles of white tinder, rot steadily in their muddy alcohol": a grotesque image which perfectly conveys the constancy in decay, the ugliness and hopelessness of the little town. It is a town that "lives on the dead," on dead customs, dead ideas-clearly, no better a place for Emma than Tostes.

At the "Golden Lion" we are briefly introduced to some of the principal citizens of Yonville; Madame Lefrancois, the landlady; Binet, the tax collector, a phlegmatic old soldier; Father Bournisien, the strapping red-faced village cure; Homais, the town pharmacist. We listen to a conversation between Madame Lefrancois and Homais. The complacency and banality of the latter's mind are revealed in a self-important harangue on the superiority of the religion of "Socrates, Franklin, Voltaire and Beranger" over the "superstition" of the Church; on the sublimity of worshipping the Supreme Being "in the woods and fields, or by gazing up into the vault of heaven"; on the absurdity of belief in "an old fogey of a God who walks round his garden with a stick in his hand, lodges his friends in the bellies of whales...." Homais' diatribe breaks off with the arrival of the coach bringing the Bovarys. They had been delayed by the loss of Emma's little greyhound-a fellow passenger, we are told, consoled Emma with stories of dogs who returned to their masters after long absences, over great distances.

Comment

Yonville and Homais are counterparts. The description of the town and of the latter's conversation carry the same message:

here is self-satisfied ugliness, smallness, mediocrity. Homais, however, is more than a representative of the town. As Emma is an example of "false romanticism," so Homais is a kind of "false rationalist." In him, "rationalism" - the great 18th century movement emphasizing reason and the scientific or critical method - has become narrow and conventional. His speech against established religion is a tissue of clichés; his "deism" - a belief in God derived by reason, a worship conducted without membership in any formal institution or according to any set rite-is a doctrinaire and respectable as the Church he condemns.

Emma's loss of her dog on the way to Yonville is perhaps suggestive of more serious losses to ensue. The animal was a greyhound, a rather aristocratic breed for a country doctor's wife, and it bore the exotic name "Djali." In a world where a Homais rules the roost, we cannot expect Emma's pretensions to survive for long.

CHAPTER TWO

Homais introduces himself to the Bovarys-as pharmacist, he will be the doctor's colleague. As Emma stands warming herself before the fire, she receives the admiring notice of Leon Dupuis, the young clerk of the town notary. During the dinner which follows, two separate and simultaneous conversations ensue. Homais delivers a lecture to Charles on the climate of Yonville, the conditions of medical practice, the backwardness and superstition of the inhabitants. At the same time, Emma and Leon are discovering affinities. Both adore sunsets, the sea, the mountains; both like to read; both fancy, in particular, those books which "allow the imagination to dwell on noble characters, pure affections, pictures of happiness."

Comment

There is an ironic parallel between the two conversations. In terms of intellectual worth, they are equivalent: Homais' speech epitomizes the provincial amateur scientist, while Emma and Leon represent the small town esthete or book-lover. Homais' pretentious, blundering discourse sounds like a **parody** of an encyclopedic article. (He erroneously converts Centigrade into Fahrenheit, and garbles an account of the generation of "noxious exhalations.") Emma and Leon exchange the tritest **clichés** of sentimental literature, outlining, in effect, the principles of false romantic taste.

The two assume that certain spectacles are intrinsically "uplifting." Possessing the desired romantic qualities of wildness, immensity, power, the mountains or sea must inevitably arouse the spectator to a sense of "the infinite, the ideal." If such emotions are not forthcoming, the false romantic will force or fake them. On the other hand, they will uniformly reject the small-in-scale, the down-to-earth: as Emma says, "I hate commonplace heroes and moderate feelings such as are to be found in life." Emma and Leon cannot fail to be sympathetic: their high-flown phrases and opinions are parroted from the same books.

The conversation continues through the evening. As Leon talks to Emma of Paris, of the new plays, novels, dances, he unconsciously puts his foot on the bar of her chair. Finally the Bovarys retire to their new house. The rooms are chilly and unfurnished, but Emma, reflecting that it is the fourth time she has slept in a new place, is convinced that something better is now in store for her.

CHAPTER THREE

The Bovarys settle in Yonville. Emma has made a great impression on Leon, who looks for her in vain at the inn the night after their meeting. A timid, essentially colorless young man, he has never before had so intimate a conversation with a lady. Homais proves an excellent neighbor, full of advice and assistance. He has been practicing medicine without a license - an offense which has already brought him before a magistrate in Rouen - and desires to get on Charles' good side.

Charles' first weeks are gloomy. He has few patients and has spent all his savings on clothing for his wife and in moving from Tostes. Emma's pregnancy is a happy distraction. Charles finds her condition enchanting and looks forward joyously to becoming a father. Emma, too, is excited at first and curious about motherhood, but is disappointed when she cannot indulge in an elegant layette. She dreams of having a son. A male child would not be a slave to physical weakness and **conventions** like a woman. A boy-he will be dark and strong, passionate and adventurous-would afford a vicarious revenge for her female helplessness. But the child is a girl. Hearing Charles' announcement, Emma turns away and faints.

The child's christening follows. Homais, as godfather, Leon and the elder Bovarys are present. The baby is called "Berthe," after one of the young ladies at La Vaubyessard-Emma had at first considered a number of aristocratic, Italianate names. The christening, made festive by Homais' gift of leftover syrups and confections from his shop and songs from Leon and Madame Bovary Senior, is almost interrupted by old Bovary's proposal to baptize the child with champagne. The old man stays in Yonville a month, running up a liquor bill in his son's name and flirting so shamelessly with his daughter-in-law that Charles' mother hastens their departure.

Comment

There is a significant contrast between Charles' and Emma's feelings on the eve of parenthood. For Charles a child will mean the completion of life: now, Flaubert says, he may settle down serenely "with both elbows firmly planted on the table of life." The image suggests Charles' stolid domesticity, his awkward manners, his lack of spirituality, and his total satisfaction. Emma, however, sees motherhood as a novel experience, an occasion for the display of style, an opportunity for vicarious fulfillment. Compared to her husband's commonplace but genuine feelings, her attitude seems frivolous and selfish. In this connection, we might also mention a familiar notion of Emma's "masculinity" of spirit. While she is "all woman" in most ways, her resentment of female subjugation, her desire to know a larger, more meaningful world, are symptoms of a "masculine" spirit. It is Charles who displays a "kitchen love," feminine domesticity, and passivity.

One day, about six weeks after Berthe's christening, Emma feels a sudden desire to see the child, who had been put out to nurse with a carpenter's wife. It is a hot, dazzling summer noon, and after walking a short distance she feels weak. She meets Leon in the village and asks him to accompany her. (The report of this will immediately spread scandal throughout Yonville.) After a walk through the hot, flowery fields, they arrive at the wet nurse's squalid cottage. Emma takes her baby in her arms, and Leon is struck by the incongruity of her beauty in such surroundings. They leave, followed briefly by the nurse, who begs for gifts of coffee and brandy.

The two walk back along the river, hemmed in by the swift, cool water and garden walls topped with broken glass and hung with honeysuckle. Emma notices the way Leon's long auburn hair falls over his velvet collar, his well cared-for nails. As they talk, they feel a strange languor stealing over them. They come to a muddy place and Emma, laughing as she leaps over stepping-stones, almost falls. She leaves Leon hurriedly at her garden gate. He walks on, feeling that he can no longer endure the boredom of Yonville, and sensing an unbridgeable abyss between himself and Emma. He would like to be intimate with her, but is too timid and inexperienced to know what to do.

Comment

Again, Flaubert uses details of the outer world to suggest the psychological state of his characters. The heat and dazzle on the day of Emma and Leon's excursion are both actual causes and symbolic counterparts of the languor and illusion which come over them. The river, streaming with weeds and little bubbles, harmonizes with the "deep continuous murmur of their souls" in which they find their whispers "drowning." The hot garden walls suggest the Yonville world which hems them in and virtually forces them together. Out of the wall grow faded flowers which Emma shatters with her parasol. Her passage over the stepping-stones suggests the danger of a moral fall, and so on.

Emma and Leon, without quite knowing it, are falling in love, and it is exactly this tenuousness and uncertainty of their feelings which leads Flaubert to render them by external detail, by suggestion rather than explicit analysis. It is noteworthy, too, that this first private meeting of Emma and Leon occurs on a visit to her baby: a fact which must emphasize for Leon the obstacles to any real intimacy with Emma, and which should also make the reader clearly aware of the impropriety of Emma's feelings.

CHAPTER FOUR

At dinnertime Homais often visits the Bovarys. Inevitably he discusses the contents of the newspaper which, complete with editorial opinion, he had memorized. That subject thoroughly dissected, he proceeds to comment on the meal, emphasizing the chemical aspects of cookery and giving a master-chef's advice to Emma and the maid, Felicite. Justin, Homais' assistant, also likes to frequent the doctor's house and the pharmacist believes he is in love with Felicite.

On Sunday evenings the Bovarys attend the pharmacist's weekly gatherings. Leon is always there and, after a game of cards, he and Emma move apart from the others to peruse a fashion magazine, to recite poetry, and to whisper while Charles and Homais fall asleep before the fire. From her parlor window Emma sees Leon pass twice a day, and from the upper stories they watch each other tend their potted plants: cactuses, the latest craze. At a third window in Yonville "still more frequently occupied" is M. Binet working at his lathe; the monotonous drone of his machine can be heard throughout the town.

When Emma makes a pretty rug for Leon people begin to think she must be his mistress. After all, he is always praising her. Leon wishes she were but is afraid to make a declaration. As for Emma, she doesn't question whether she is in love. She believes that love must take you by storm and does not realize that it can come quietly and imperceptibly into a life.

Comment

The love between Emma and Leon, still in the latent stage for her, ripens naturally as the life of Yonville continually throws them together. The "exalted" sympathy between them is juxtaposed to the more mundane interests of the other characters. Again, as in the simultaneous conversations in Chapter Two, Flaubert uses the technique of ironically commenting upon one action by describing another that occurs at the same time. Thus, Leon declaims romantic verses with Emma while Homais' dominoes rattle in the background. In the fair scene (Part Two, Chapter Eight) we will see this device more fully exploited.

CHAPTER FIVE

One snowy afternoon in February Homais takes his children, Napoleon and Athalie, with Leon, Justin, and the Bovarys, to see a new flax-mill under construction outside Yonville. Nothing could be less interesting, but Homais lectures at length about its importance to the town and the strength of its beams. Emma, bored, gazes at the misty sky, then begins to study the appearance of her husband and Leon. With a sense of revelation, she notes the contrast between them. Charles, thick lips trembling, cap pulled down over his eyes, looks incredibly stupid, while Leon, pale and languorous, with soulful big blue eyes, seems ideally sensitive. That evening the contrast recurs to Emma with intense clarity, leading her to trace in memory her entire acquaintance with Leon. Suddenly, she recognizes that he must be in love with her! She is possessed at once of a new joy . . . and a new frustration.

Comment

The setting in which Emma first views Leon with eyes of love is one designed to make her feel acutely the bleakness of her life. It is winter, the dead season; the site of the mill is a large piece of waste ground strewn with rubble. (Homais, of course, only regards as a triumph of progress that industrial ugliness which will ultimately claim little Berthe, who as an impoverished orphan will go to work in such a mill), Leon's almost feminine delicacy provides Emma with a welcome contrast not only to Charles' stolid masculinity but to the general drabness of the environment.

The next evening Emma has a visit from the draper, M. Lheureux, a fat, swarthy man with unpleasantly sharp little eyes, who is always bent over in a kind of bow. He is known as a sly fellow. He introduces himself with a stream of flattering phrases and assures Madame that though his own shop is modest, he has contacts with all the leading merchants of Rouen and can get her anything she might desire. He just happens to have with him some pretty embroidered collars, imported scarves, and coconut-shell egg-cups. When Emma hesitantly declines these goods, Lheureux makes a startling suggestion. Assuming an air by turns obsequious, good-natured, conspiratorial, he tells her that, if the need should arise, he could lend her money.

Comment

Lheureux will play a diabolical part in Emma's ruin and is portrayed with many traditional attributes of the devil or tempter. He is dark and foreign in appearance, with a mysterious past; a smooth talker, he has an intuition for secret desires, especially those of the "ladies." Leading Emma deeper and deeper into debt and deception he will, in effect, exact the price of her soul through moral decay and suicide. His name, both ironically and properly, means the "happy" or "fortunate" one; his kind of ruthless acquisitiveness is irresistibly successful in Yonville and 19th century France.

When Leon comes to visit, Emma makes a great show of being a loving and virtuous wife and mother. She praises her husband, takes a great interest in domestic duties, attends church regularly, and, whenever there are guests, displays a rapturous pride in her little girl. Confronted with this spectacle of marital bliss, Leon's discouraged love becomes refined of fleshly desires, grows pure, platonic. Emma, pale, quiet, enigmatic, gives the impression of a saint, while her heart is in turmoil. The more in love she is with Leon, the more she tries to suppress it. At first there is some consolation in saying "I am a virtuous woman," but soon her longing for love, her craving for money, and her myriad domestic discontents combine in one general feeling of misery and rage.

Charles, the cause her unhappiness, has no idea that she is suffering. In his complacency he believes that he makes her completely happy. She wishes that Charles would beat her so that she would have an excuse for hatred and revenge. She thinks of running away with Leon. "but at once a vague , dark chasm yawned within her soul." In public she continues to smile, while alone in her room she has fits of hysterical weeping.

CHAPTER SIX

One evening early in April, Emma looks out at the countryside beyond Yonville. Spring flowers are blossoming; the river winds among the meadows; a violet haze hangs among lifeless poplars.

The Angelus rings, transporting her back to the convent of her girlhood. She sees herself among the nuns at Sunday mass, one of the girls in white veils; remembers the altar with its flowers and tall candlesticks, the fumes of incense rising before the statue of the Virgin. Drawn by an impulse to dissolve her being and troubles in worship, she finds hurrying to the church.

Comment

Almost every detail of the actual scene at Yonville is related to one or more details of the remembered scene at the convent. The gardens full of flowers suggest the altar or the girls in their Sunday finery. The leafless poplars resemble the altar candles or the columns of the tabernacle. The evening mist is like the haze of incense or the veils of the girls. A summoning bell rings throughout both scenes. These correspondences not only illustrate Flaubert's idea of the way memory operates, but fuse two traditional images of peace and innocence: a rural landscape and a convent service. Joined, the two scenes emphasize all the more strongly Emma's loss of peace and innocence.

Children waiting for their catechism class are playing among the dusty tombstones beside the church. Father Bournisien-ruddy, full-fed, in a cassock stained by food and tobacco-emerges from the vicarage. Emma tries to reveal her unhappiness.

She says she feels dreadful; he attributes it to the unseasonable heat. She remarks that he, as a priest, heals all ills; yes, he agrees, citing a recent visit to a sick cow. Farmers have a hard time, he says; yes, she replies, but they're not the only ones. He agrees: There are workers in town and poor mothers with families. She observes that some people have bread, but lack . . . "a good fire in winter," he suggests. Emma gives up the idea of talking to him. As she leaves, she hears the children repeating their catechism: "A Christian is one who being baptized . . . baptized . . . baptized. . . ."

Comment

The shabby little church of Yonville is very different from the chapel of the fashionable convent of Emma's memory. The priest, too, hardly answers to Emma's needs. Abbe Bournisien epitomizes the shortcomings of the provincial clergy. The higher functions of his calling have been lost in a round of practical duties. He is so lacking in imagination and genuine spiritual insight that when Emma suggests-in effect -that men do not live by bread alone, he says, yes, they need a good fire. This reply, made without a trace of conscious **irony**, completely contradicts the spirit of his religion. Bournisien, though a priest, hardly recognizes the existence of "soul." All problems, for him are material, with such causes as weather, poverty, diet, or disease. Thus, when Emma comes seeking the mystic sustenance of faith, he recommends a good cup of tea. The children's voices Emma hears as she walks away suggest that the people of Yonville get no further in their understanding of what Christianity means than knowing a Christian is baptized . . .baptized . . .baptized.

Disconsolate, Emma returns home. When little Berthe tries to play with her, she pushes the child away, accidentally cutting its cheek. At first she feels guilt and anxiety, then-after Charles assures her the injury is minor-congratulates herself on her display of maternal concern. She stares at the sleeping child's tear-stained face and is struck by how "ugly" it is.

We learn, after a discussion between Charles and Homais on the subject of childhood accidents and their prevention, that Leon has at last resolved to leave Yonville. Boredom and frustration have overpowered his hopes of Emma and her fear of change. He imagines himself in Paris, living like an artist, dancing at masked balls and courting the shop girls. After many delays and the preparation of an elaborate "outfit," the day of his departure arrives.

Leon calls on the Bovarys. He and Emma - Charles is not at home - exchange only trivial remarks, but every word is charged with the anguish of departure, their undeclared love. Leon kisses Berthe, shakes Emma's hand - thrilling at this physical contact - and runs down the street to the waiting carriage.

For a long time Emma stands at her window. A storm comes up over Rouen, then the sun comes out again. She thinks of how far away Leon must already be. After dinner Homais drops by, and he and Charles discuss their young friend's prospects in Paris. Homais speaks of the gay life of the students and the scoundrels who lie in wait for a country boy. Charles is concerned about the possibility of disease. Emma's only contribution to the discussion is an occasional sigh or shudder. Homais leaves, mentioning that the annual regional agricultural fair will probably be held in Yonville that year.

Comment

The scene of Leon and Emma's parting is notable for its austere objectivity: the "lovers" do not declare themselves, nor does Flaubert attempt to analyze their feelings. Their conduct is underscored by the excessively tearful farewell of Homais, who cares relatively little for Leon. Afterwards, too, there is little explicit revelation of Emma's feelings; Flaubert does not wish to spoil the effect of the lovers' reticence. Only the storm serves as a direct symbol of her emotions; though, during Charles and Homais' later discussion of Leon, we are constantly aware of what her reactions must be.

CHAPTER SEVEN

The period following Leon's departure is one of desolation and mourning for Emma. The scenes that witnessed their friendship perpetually "recall the image of a taller, handsomer . . . and vaguer Leon." She regrets her virtuous silence and lost opportunity, and even thinks of running after him to declare her love. Little by little, however, the fire of her passion dies- whether, as Flaubert says, "from an insufficiency or an overload of fuel," from Leon's absence or her desperate efforts to feed her grief. A wintry night of feelings succeeds, in which Emma, to compensate for her "sacrifice," indulges herself in luxuries of dress and cosmetics; changes her hair style; and undertakes the study of Italian, history and philosophy. All her projects are soon dropped, however, and she grows more capricious, fretful, and pale. Charles' mother, called into consultation by her worried son, suggests hard work as a cure and tries to cut off Emma's supply of "wicked" novels.

Comment

Emma's feelings after Leon's departure are strikingly similar to her mood after the ball at La Vaubyessard: this, too, has made a "gap in her life." She suffers the same dreariness and self-abandonment, the vain distractions, the failure of health. The actual winter of Tostes is paralleled by the metaphors of darkness and winter which describe her feelings at Yonville. However, while her love for Leon fades, it gives her melancholy a new focus. At Tostes she neglected her appearance, gave up her music and drawing; at Yonville on the contrary, her dress becomes more elaborate and she tries to acquire new accomplishments. A central image in this chapter is Emma reclining on her sofa in the afternoon, wearing her dressing gown and new sash, elaborately coiffured, a novel in her hand: like a woman waiting for her lover. After Leon, she is unconsciously preparing to take a lover, and, as Flaubert remarks-alluding to her drinking a whole glass of brandy on a dare from Charles-she now needs "little encouragement to grow quite wild."

One market day a gentleman and his servant call at the Bovarys. The servant wishes to be bled for some fancied ailment. During the operation he faints, as does Justin, Homais' young apprentice who has been assisting Charles. In the confusion that follows both Homais and Emma lend a hand-Emma appearing to particular advantage as she kneels in her summer dress beside the swooning boy. The gentleman, one Rodolphe Boulanger, the new proprietor of the neighboring estate of La Huchette, is a bachelor of thirty-four. Handsome, shrewd, unburdened by any delicacy of conscience or feelings, Boulanger is tiring of his current mistress, an actress in Rouen. He is struck by Emma's gracefulness and gentility, her pallor and dark eyes. With the clarity born of much experience with women, he sums up Emma's case: obviously, she's bored to death, disgusted with her lout of a husband, yearning for excitement and love: "Three pretty words and she'd adore you." It would be so easy. A visit or two, a few gifts of game or poultry to the Bovarys, an invitation . . . He resolves to make her his mistress. In a few days the fair will be held, a good time, he thinks, to start.

CHAPTER EIGHT

It is the day of the fair. A crowd begins to gather: women in starched bonnets and bright kerchiefs; men smocks and frock coats; the local militia in red and black. Stands have been erected; banners and ivy adorn the facade of the Town Hall; tricolors hang from the windows. Homais bustles by, pausing to deliver a lecture on the connection between chemistry and farming to Madame Lefrancois. Emma strolls past on Rodolphe Boulanger's arm.

Rodolphe has been trying to get Emma alone and in intimate conversation. By flattering her and ridiculing the other Yonville ladies, a certain sympathy is established. They talk of the crushing dullness of the country, and Rodolphe confesses that he is sinking into a state of gloom. Emma is surprised; she had thought him cheerful. He assures her it is only a "jester's mask," that often he has grim thoughts in moonlit graveyards. He has no friends; he is all alone. If only he had an aim in life, someone to love him!

The principal speaker arrives, one of the prefect's deputies. Drums beat; the guard of honor is mustered; a cannon booms. As the speakers and the committee mount the platform, Emma and Rodolphe ascend to the vantage point of the empty council chamber of the Town Hall.

Comment

Like the description of Emma's wedding, the fair reveals Flaubert's pictorial skill. He has a painter's eye for color and contrast, for typical costume and expressive gesture. The visual is augmented by sound and smell, and often many effects are combined in a single image. Consider, for instance, "Now and then a door-knocker banged back behind a lady in cotton gloves . . ." There is the coincidence of quick back-swing and thud, the little shock it must give to the propriety of such a lady as wears cotton gloves, the sense that on such a day of festivity there will be many little shocks to propriety. Particularly significant is Flaubert's description of the animals at the fair: that "undulating tide of massed beasts" peaked by the jut of horns or a flowing white mane. These, with the restive stallions and the motionless black bull, suggest the wave of animal desire rising in Emma and Rodolphe.

The deputy's speech opens, predictably, with praise of the king and the new era of peace and prosperity, then extols the patriotism and usefulness of the farmer, and concludes with an exhortation to continue the good work under the blessing of an all-wise, benevolent government. Simultaneously, Rodolphe is trying his "line" on Emma.

As the deputy alludes to bad old days of strife and bloodshed, Rodolphe mentions his bad reputation, the inevitable consequence of his soul's shuttling between a passion for purity and orgies of self-indulgence. He still believes in the possibility of happiness, however. Just when you despair of it, the destined lover will appear, and the soul will step "out of darkness into light." To illustrate his **metaphor**, he passes his hand across his face, then lets it fall on Emma's. She withdraws hers.

The deputy lauds the intelligence of the farmer - not vain "superficial intelligence," but service of the common good and respect for duty. Duty, Rodolphe echoes, what does it mean? Our only duty is to feel nobly and to love what is beautiful. When Emma demurs, he insists there are two moralities: the petty conventional morality of the mob and the "eternal" morality of passion. Pure souls sealed to the latter, he adds, may be persecuted by the mob, but their love must be fulfilled, since "Fate" ordains it. Fascinated by his speech, breathing the perfume of his hair, Emma half forgets where she is: she is waltzing with the Viscount at La Vaubyessard, Leon is next to her . . . "Keep steadily ahead!" cries the voice of the deputy.

A second dignitary begins a speech on farming and religion, the props of civilization. As he speaks of primitive pre-agricultural society, Roman generals and Chinese emperors, Rodolphe talks to Emma of dreams, presentiments, mysterious affinities originating out of previous existences. He takes her hand again, and she does not withdraw it. The prize-giving commences. Rodolphe's words are continually broken by the announcements of the judges. The last award-as Rodolphe squeezes Emma's hand and she returns the pressure- is made to an old woman for fifty-four years of continuous domestic service. Reduced by her years of servitude to a kind of selfless husk, the old woman timorously accepts her silver medal and walks off muttering that she will give it to the priest to say mass for her.

Comment

In Part One, Chapter Two, we have already seen Flaubert's use of simultaneous conversations for the sake of ironic contrast, but here the effect is sharper and more complex. There is an overall kinship between the two streams of speech (Rodolphe's and the orators') in terms of intellectual value, tone, general method and purpose, and effect. Both are a mishmash of clichés, one of political oratory, the other of romance. (Consider the deputy's ludicrous mixed **metaphor** of the king steering "the chariot of state . . . amid the ceaseless perils of a stormy sea . . . ," or Rodolphe's seducer's vocabulary of "nobility", "purity," "Fate.") The method of both is flattery, to obtain love or allegiance. The tone of both is inflated and insincere; and both enthrall their audience.

Beyond this general similarity, moreover, the two streams of speech are linked to each other in detail: sometimes by way of direct inspiration, as when Rodolphe gets the clue for his remarks on "duty" from the deputy's speech; more often by a relationship in tone, as when Rodolphe's upbeat on the possibility of happiness is followed by the deputy's paean to the patriotic farmer. This kind of point-by-point correspondence reaches its ironic height during the prize-giving, when interruptions of the judges emphasize the hollowness and falsity of Rodolphe's words. Thus, when Rodolphe tells Emma that only destiny is responsible for their rendezvous, a voice cries "Seventy francs!" like a prostitute or her customer setting the price of an assignation; when he tells her that he couldn't keep away though he tried a hundred times, the mocking voice retorts "Manure!"

The viciousness and superficiality of both sets of speakers, of the ruling conventions-both public and private-of Flaubert's France, are underlined by the appearance of the old woman. For her lifetime of sacrifice she receives the callous compensation of a prize worth twenty-five francs, for which she can find no other use than to pay for masses after she is dead. Wrinkled, shriveled, mute as a beast, she is the victim of (and judgement upon) a world in which the catch-words of romance, patriotism, progress, are masks for selfishness and exploitation.

The fair concludes with a gross and noisy banquet, followed by a display of fireworks, most of which fail to go off because of dampness. Emma and Rodolphe have no opportunity to converse, beyond a tender glance or two, after their meeting in the council chamber. Two days later, an article on the fair written by Homais appears in the Rouen paper. It is a masterpiece of florid provincial journalism, replete with the deadliest rhetorical phrases (the martial bearing of our militia, "our sprightly village lasses"), shameless puffs of his own reputation (as one of the judges, as author of a treatise on cider), and blatant fabrications (the abortive fireworks display was a "veritable kaleidoscope").

CHAPTER NINE

Six weeks elapse before Rodolphe revisits Emma. He has calculated that if she really cares for him delay is strategic. The moment he sees her, pale and silent in her sitting room, he knows he was right. He apologizes for his presence, for his absence. He tried to keep away, for she bears another's name, but he could not fight fate and irresistible charm; even during the weeks of absence he has come night after night to gaze at her house. Charles enters, and Rodolphe, improvising, says that they have been talking about Emma's health. He proposes riding as a therapy and offers to put a horse at her disposal. Emma declines. Later, she tells Charles that it wouldn't "look right," and besides, she has no riding-habit. Charles insists that appearances are unimportant: health comes first, and he will buy her a riding-habit. This decides her.

Several days later, on a misty afternoon in early October, Rodolphe arrives at the Bovarys with two saddle-horses-Charles having written that his wide awaits Rodolphe's "convenience." The two mount their animals and, after a farewell to little Berthe at the window and a warning from Homais against "accidents," they canter off to the hill.

From the hilltop the misty valley looks like a white lake. In intervals of sunshine Emma can see Yonville: it never looked so tiny. They ride on, entering the forest. The air is warm; the red-brown earth soft beneath the horse's hooves. Rodolphe often comes abreast of Emma to free her stirrup from entangling ferns or to push back branches. The sun comes out, reviving the rich autumnal colors: violet of heather, gray, fawn gold. The two dismount and walk along a footpath. Behind a long blue veil, Emma's face looks as though it were "floating beneath azure waves."

In a clearing Rodolphe declares his love, calmly and seriously, so as not to alarm Emma. She implores him to let her go: it cannot be; he frightens her. She has the wrong idea, he says. To him, she is a "Madonna on a pedestal . . . high, secure and immaculate." Only, he cannot live without her . . . as a friend, a sister. His arm is around her; he implores her to stay. Crying "It's wrong, wrong!" she leans against his shoulder, bends back her white throat, and surrenders.

Afterwards, all is transformed for Emma. "Sweetness seemed to breathe from the trees." All is silence, except for a strange cry dying away beyond the woods. The low sun is brilliant. Following their own tracks, they ride out of the woods, Rodolphe bending now and then to kiss Emma's hand. In the evening, she escapes Charles early and goes up to her room to reenact in imagination the scenes of the afternoon. She stares at herself in the mirror: never have her eyes appeared so big and dark. She feels she has entered, after years of suffering, into her girlhood dream-world of passion and bliss, joined the "lyrical legion of adulteresses," heroines of romantic novels. She seems to stand on a height overlooking ordinary life, with a "misty blue immensity" about her. Again and again she says to herself, "I've a lover, a lover."

Comment

It is significant that the seduction takes place during an outing on horseback. Rodolphe, with his shiny boots and gaiters, has been associated with horsemanship as, indeed, are all his class (see Part One, Chapter Eight). It is part of the aristocrat's chivalric heritage, and an ironic measure of his decline that now the horse is merely an instrument of recreation, wager or, as in this case, seduction. As for Emma, who has cherished from her girlhood the image of the white-plumed cavalier, her dream has come true; she has been carried off by a knight on horseback. The whole **episode**, in fact , is a kind of **parody** of that stock romantic scene: for the "knight" is a hard-hearted vulgar seducer and the "lady" the disgruntled wife of a country doctor.

We may also note, aside from the "horse" motif, a continuation of the animal **theme** of the preceding chapter. Here it is the small furtive creatures of the underbrush whose alarms lead them further into the forest, as a tremulous Emma allows herself to be lured deeper into the wild. All around her is the stir of life, and thick growth catching at her, hemming her in . Finally, we should catch the repeated references to mist or haze: the mist which hides the valley; Emma's veil, like a "haze of blue"; and the "misty blue immensity" of her rapture. These images suggest not only a world which is transfigured by romantic illusions, but perhaps the obscurity of Emma's motives: essentially she allows herself to be so quickly seduced by Rodolphe as a "reward" for her virtue with Leon.

Days of delight follow. In a hut in the forest Emma tells Rodolphe of her sorrows, receives his vows and kisses. Each night they leave letters for each other in a crevice of the garden wall. Emma acquires the habit of visiting Rodolphe at his estate, La Huchette, before daybreak. Breathless and flushed, she arrives "like a spring morning," to fall into his arms. One day-she cannot keep away-she arrives unexpectedly and Rodolphe frowns. She is becoming reckless, he says, and is compromising herself.

Comment

Emma's impetuous and sincere passion is contrasted to Rodolphe's calculating dalliance. Already, we begin to see that avoiding "trouble" will be more important for him than Emma herself. True, in the seduction scene we are aware of the dual nature of Emma's motives: from the beginning, she hopes for and expects Rodolphe's advances, then makes a pretense of mystification and rejection. But this normal ambivalence of a woman in love does not nullify her sincerity. The harshest **irony** is reserved for Rodolphe, the kind of man who fondles a woman at the very moment of calling her an immaculate "Madonna." With all the elements of **parody** in the seduction scene, we must believe that something genuine has happened to Emma: her sense of a sweet union with nature after the love-making seems an unmistakable guarantee of this. Her later sense of sisterhood with the literary adulteresses may elicit Flaubert's scorn, but he is too much a romantic to repudiate an identification with nature - the natural - as distinct from books. It is the natural in Emma, as much as her affectations, that will tire Rodolphe.

MADAME BOVARY

. . . .

CHAPTER TEN

As Emma becomes more involved in her affair, she grows obsessed by the thought of difficulties arising, particularly discovery. One morning as she is crossing the fields after a rendezvous, she runs into Binet, the tax-collector. He is almost as alarmed as she; he has been hunting duck illegally and is on the lookout for police. "You're out early?" he says. "Yes," she falters, "I've been to the nurse's, to see my baby." Then she rudely cuts off further conversation and walks away. Immediately she regrets her transparent lie. Everyone knows her child has been home for over a year, and the path leads only to La Huchette. That evening at Homais' she sees Binet again, but his one innuendo on their encounter escapes Charles. To be safe Emma and Rodolphe arrange more discreet assignations.

During the winter, three or four times a week, Rodolphe comes to Emma's garden in the dead of night. When Charles is asleep Emma slips out, trembling, half-undressed. In the dark, cold nights the lovers cling together, their sighs magnified. Shadows "shudder and lean over like immense black waves advancing to engulf them." On rainy nights they take shelter in Charles' consulting room, which Rodolphe finds very amusing. When Emma suggests that he bring pistols to defend himself should Charles discover them, Rodolphe laughs, "Your husband? Ha! Poor little man!"

Rodolphe finds Emma's sentimentality as ridiculous as her melodrama. They have to exchange portraits, locks of hair; she wants a ring as a symbol of their "lifelong union"; she constantly uses such phrases as "voices of nature" and "bells of evening." Previously Rodolphe's affairs have been merely lustful adventures. Emma's emotionalism is a new experience that both flatters him and arouses his common-sense disdain. Once sure of her love, his attitude toward her grows careless and indifferent. Emma is astonished to find the grand passion dwindling. She feels humiliated, then bitter. Desperately, she redoubles her tenderness.

Comment

Instead of freeing, Emma's love subjugates her. She is at the mercy of her newly awakened sensuality, Rodolphe's hardheartedness, and her fears. Even a fool like Binet can be dangerous. As the affair progresses joy gives way to guilty desperation. Accordingly, the lovers no longer meet by day, in the sunlight, but at night in cold, menacing darkness. Rodolphe provides a new view of Emma. To her husband, her neighbors and herself she seemed clever and worldly. To Rodolphe, however, she is a naive and artless creature. Though wealthy and sophisticated, Rodolphe is essentially as unromantic as any bourgeois. His shallow soul is mystified and shocked by Emma's naive demonstrativeness.

At the end of the winter M. Rouault sends his annual turkey (to commemorate Charles' mending of his broken leg) and with it a loving letter that moves Emma to reminisce fondly on the days of her girlhood. "Happy days . . . rich in illusions!" She has no illusions now. She has spent them all on the various adventures of her life and has been left unhappy. Why? Her sadness inspires a rush of tenderness for little Berthe, and a sudden coldness toward Rodolphe, Rodolphe ignores it. Then Emma repents; she wonders, at last, whether she couldn't try to love Charles, to do something for him. This proves to be very difficult until Homais makes a suggestion that seems to provide her with an opportunity.

Comment

Emma's repentance, her tenderness toward her child, and her wish to show Charles some affection reflect a pathetic desire to regain innocence. The same desire prompts her to think fondly of her father and to remember her early youth in golden images. In terms of what is to follow, this change of heart must be viewed as more ironic than pathetic, a routine "phase" of illicit love.

CHAPTER ELEVEN

Homais has read of a wonderful new treatment for clubfeet and is eager to try the operation on Hippolyte, the crippled groom at the Golden Lion. Perhaps, Emma thinks, her husband may be a good surgeon and a cure will bring them fame and fortune. She and Homais persuade Charles to undertake the treatment and, by offering it free, by flattery and scolding, win the groom's consent.

The operation seems to go well, though Charles, always uncertain of his skill, has been in doubt as to what class of clubfoot Hippolyte's belongs. The Achilles tendon is cut, the foot fastened into a heavy box of wood and iron, and the triumphant Charles returns home to his wife's embrace. All evening they talk of their coming good fortune. Emma regales herself with the new, the "finer, more wholesome delight" of marital affection. She even notices that Charles' teeth are "not too bad." Homais drops by with the manuscript of a newspaper article lauding Charles as a hero of progress and philanthropy.

Five days later, however, Hippolyte is screaming with pain. The box is removed, but as soon as the swelling of the foot subsides, is clamped on tighter than before to speed the cure. In another three days, the continued agonies of the groom compel Charles and Homais to remove the apparatus for good. By this time the club-foot's leg is obviously gangrenous. For days he lies on the billiard table of the Golden Lion, a spectacle and victim of all sorts of conflicting advice. The priest, Father Bournisien, is a frequent visitor, exhorting Hippolyte to change his ways, undertake new duties and vows. Finally, they are forced to call in another doctor, a famous, rough-spoken, old-fashioned physician named Canivet, who jeers at such efforts to improve on nature and declares that a high amputation is now necessary.

The next day the operation takes place, Homais-who made no effort to defend Charles-assisting. Charles sits at home, ashamed to go out, trying to figure where he went wrong, envisioning the scandal and ruin to come. Emma stares at him. How could she have expected anything from such a man? A horrible scream rises from the inn and Charles turns pale. Emma bitterly recalls her sacrifices, her penitence-all for a man incapable of feeling, of even realizing that now she must share the ridicule attached to his name. A series of prolonged wails "like the howling of some animal being slaughtered in the distance" break the silence. Everything about Charles is odious. Vengefully she returns to thoughts of her lover, to the "malicious ironies of adultery triumphant." In his misery Charles begs the comfort of a kiss. "Let me alone!" she screams and runs out of the room. That evening when she meets Rodolphe the two recapture the first intensity of their passion.

Comment

Central to this chapter is the idea of the cruelty of "benevolence" which is selfishly motivated and has no real charity for its object: nothing could be more like torture than the "humanity" and "science" inflicted upon Hippolyte. Emma and Homais desire Charles to undertake the operation largely for the glory that may accrue to themselves. There is little genuine concern for Charles, and virtually none for the poor clubfoot. Beyond this, the barbarity of unenlightened "benevolence" is illustrated by the priest, who exploits agony and terror as an opportunity for conversion. The chapter thus gives expression to Flaubert's scepticism of science, philanthropy and organized religion: the three forces which the 19th century viewed as irresistibly leading to human betterment.

Charles, too, is a victim of selfish "benevolence." There is a close parallel between the operation and the evolution of Emma's feelings toward her husband. The attempt to change the cripple's physical condition is analogous to Emma's effort to alter her image of Charles, and both operations end in the same kind of disaster. The two developments coincide chronologically, too. At the very moment that Hippolyte is losing his leg, Charles loses, forever, his last hold on his wife's respect and affection. It is notable, incidentally, that at this terrible moment Emma, looking at Charles, hasn't the slightest sense of his sufferings, feels not a trace of remorse or responsibility. Here, for the first time, Emma is hateful. The chapter, with its gruesome, black humor, warning whiff of physical decays, is a major turning-point in the book. Henceforth, Emma's course runs more decidedly downward to corruption and death.

CHAPTER TWELVE

Emma's love for Rodolphe, nourished by her loathing of Charles, becomes more passionate and self-abandoned. To enhance her attractiveness to her lover she spends lavishly on gifts, cosmetics, jewelry and clothing. All day Felicite, the maid, washes and irons her under-linen while young Justin, who secretly worships Emma, looks on with fascination. As for Rodolphe, Emma's gifts embarrass him, her romantic whims confuse him, her adoration baffles him, and her frequent proposals of elopement strike him as insane and inconvenient. However, while their affair has lost much of its novelty, it still has some new pleasures for him. Emma has become so doting and dependent that he can do with her as he pleases: she has become "corrupt and pliant . . . a thing of idiocy...."

Comment

The new intensity of Emma's love is actually symptomatic of its decay. It is an unhealthy passion, feverish, overripe. She no longer finds in it the rapturous fulfillment of a dream, but a kind of sensual oblivion, a "drugged blessedness." Hers is a voluptuousness born of despair and, though she cannot admit it, despair of Rodolphe as well as Charles, for she must realize that her lover is far less committed than she. Her slavishness may be interpreted as an attempt to propitiate and bind him.

Yet, however corrupt, Emma's love remains genuine. What Rodolphe cannot understand when she says "there are women more beautiful than I, but none that can love as I can. I am your slave, your concubine. You are my king, my idol ..." is that there is real passion behind these high-flown phrases. The words of love are always the same, Flaubert says, and the most sincere heart may resort to the emptiest metaphors, for "human speech is like a cracked kettle on which we strum out tunes to make a bear dance, when we would move the stars to pity."

Emma's shamelessness becomes open and public. She goes so far as to appear in the streets with a cigarette in her mouth, or "squeezed into a waistcoat, like a man." Her extravagance puts her deeply into debt to Lheureux, but she is able to extricate herself by purloining one of Charles' fees. The payment obviously disappoints Lheureux, who hopes to get Emma into his power. A crisis arises during a visit of Charles' mother, who is shocked by the new "tone" of the Bovary household and suspicious of her daughter-in-law's virtue. A bitter quarrel breaks out between the two women, and in the end Emma, persuaded by Charles, resentfully apologizes. Afterwards, she sends for Rodolphe and, flinging herself into his arms, cries that she can no longer endure it, begs him to save her, to take her away. Moved by her beauty and grief, he assents.

Comment

It is interesting that Emma's rebellious displays-the smoking, the waistcoat-have a masculine character, as if inspired by envy of the relative freedom of men, or in emulation of her lover. Even more than in such recklessness, however, Emma's deepening corruption is shown in her growing bondage to Lheureux and the desperate shifts to which it leads her. Lheureux is a man who seems almost less motivated by greed than a malevolent hunger for power, who desires the ruin and humiliation of his debtors even more than reimbursement. Revealing is the scene in which, after guessing that Emma is buying gifts for a lover, he walks off repeating, with his "habitual little hissing noise," "We shall see, we shall see!" This is the voice of the Serpent.

In the days that follow, Emma surprises her mother-in-law by her docility and quietness. Her forthcoming escape makes her indifferent to her surroundings. She has never looked so lovely, so ripe and provocative: "there was about her that indefinable beauty which comes of joy, of enthusiasm, of success. . . ." At night, Charles gazes at her with delight, then turns to look at Berthe in her cradle. He dreams of the little girl growing up, going off to school, becoming as charming as her mother, marrying some good, well-to-do young man. Charles will need money for this, of course. (Emma's expenditures have eaten up his income; he has had to buy a set of artificial legs for Hippolyte.) Perhaps he can rent a small farm, save money, increase his practice. Beside him, feigning sleep, Emma has other visions. She and Rodolphe are riding through the mountains, through marvelous cities of domes and steeples, with forests of orange trees, flowers and fountains. At last they come to a little fishing village under a cliff by the head of a bay. There, life will be "large and easy as their silken garments, all warm and starry as the soft night they would gaze upon...."

Comment

There is a striking contrast between the reveries of Charles and Emma. His, domestic and "practical," is the archetypical middle-class dream: a bit of land, money in the bank, daughter growing up, piano lessons, embroidered slippers for daddy, a respectable young man, a family line. Emma's fantasy-ironically, a virtual repetition of her honeymoon reveries (see Part One, Chapter Seven) - is the essence of romanticism. Though it may be absurdly all-encompassing and present the most incongruous features side by side: southern domes and northern steeples, orange groves and city squares with statues and fountains, the passage has extraordinary beauty and closely resembles the fanciful voyages and exotic landscapes that play a symbolic role in a number of famous French romantic poems. Flaubert emphasizes the vagueness and inactivity of this realm, but the real objection is that, while the poets used such scenes to create a merely symbolic land-of-heart's-desire, Emma means to live there.

We should also note the subtle handling of sound and feeling here: how the onward movement of the description of the journey ends, when the goal is reached, in a kind of anchored rocking rhythm, in a sense of reduplication and rest. This effect is partly created by specific images: waves, a swaying hammock, a drifting gondola, and partly by paired adjectives and phrases as in "The days, all magnificent, were all alike as waves. The vision hovered on the horizon, infinite and harmonious, in a haze of blue, in wash of sunshine. . . ." We notice, too, phrase "haze of blue" in the last sentence.

Blue is, for Emma, very much the color of happiness: we are reminded of the blue of silk blinds diffused through her honeymoon revery, the "misty-blue immensity" of her rapture after the seduction.

Emma orders a traveling-cloak and luggage from Lheureux. Rodolphe has supposedly arranged for passports and passage to Marseilles. Emma at first told him they must take Berthe, but for weeks nothing has been said of this. The night before their departure is scheduled, Rodolphe meets Emma. He is strangely melancholy and tender. A full moon rises, flooding the landscape with light, and Emma thinks of all the glorious nights to come. She will cling to Rodolphe; she will be everything to him, lover, family, country; each day will bring them closer and closer. After they part, Rodolphe stares for a moment at her vanishing white form and almost swoons with nostalgic tenderness for her. But it would be "too stupid" to flee the country and saddling himself with a child and expenses. "All the same," he says, "she was a pretty mistress."

CHAPTER THIRTEEN

At home, Rodolphe sits down to write a letter of farewell, but has difficulty thinking what to say. Emma already seems so far away. To refresh his memory and inspiration, he pulls out a biscuit-tin stuffed with old letters and trophies of love: garters, dried bouquets, locks of hair. Idly shuffling the letters from hand to hand, he recalls (very imperfectly) some of his former mistresses. Finally bored, he remarks "What a lot of humbug!" and turns to Emma's letter. He urges to be brave; says he does not want to ruin her life. Think of the humiliation she might be exposed to-she, whom he would set on a throne!-or the possibility of their love fading, her remorse. The thought of her suffering is torture to him. She must forget him, but not blame him. "No, by heavens; blame only Fate!" He will leave the country as penance for the harm he has done. He begs her to remember him, to have her child pray for him. It's a well-composed letter, he thinks, garnishing it with a few drops from a glass of water-for tears. He smokes three pipes and goes to bed.

Comment

Rodolphe's callousness and hypocrisy are evident in every practiced **cliché** of his letter, in his pose of heroic self-sacrifice. "Humbug" sums up his libertine's view of love: "for his pleasures had so trampled on his heart ... that no green thing could grow there." He has little feeling for the pain he will cause Emma; it's the thought that she may account the jilting to cheapness that really disturbs him. At such junctures in his life, as when he set out to seduce Emma (Part Two, Chapter Eight), Rodolphe finds it convenient to blame his actions on "Fate" - as he says, "Always an effective word." Fate, for him, is the shoehorn of seduction, and just as serviceable in getting out of love as getting in.

The letter is delivered to Emma in a basket of apricots carried by a peasant, a device Rodolphe has used before. As soon as she sees the man, Emma knows something is wrong. Clutching the letter, she runs upstairs to the attic and drags herself to the shuttered window. It is stiflingly hot under the slates, and the empty square glitters in the sun. The only sound is the droning of Binet's lathe. The letter fills Emma with hysterical rage and confusion. She imagines herself in Rodolphe's arms; she feels her heart pounding against her ribs; the room spins round. Why not have done with it, she thinks, leaning toward the window. The earth seems to sway up to her, the sky presses down, "the air was circling in her hollow head ... And all the time the lathe went on whirring, whirring, like a voice furiously calling her." Then Charles calls her: dinner is being served.

Comment

This scene, which is the first exhibition of the suicide impulse in Emma, gives a particularly vivid impression of the physical factors supporting the impulse: the intolerable heat and stuffiness of the attic, the empty glare outside. In fact, the drive to suicide is rendered not so much by Emma's own voice crying "Go on! Go on!" as by the animating of the physical surroundings, the tilting floor, the down-pressing sky, and, above all, the summoning drone of Binet's lathe. Thus, Flaubert suggests the suicide's terrible helplessness at such moments, the sense that his destruction is being caused by forces outside him.

The sound of Binet's lathe, like the hum heard in a swoon, permeates the whole passage. It is the voice of Yonville: for Binet, the stiffest and most insipid figure in the town, is also, in a way, its most representative. In his hobby, the turning out of hundreds of napkin-rings, none of which he gives away, he epitomizes the Yonville bourgeoisie; the imbecile acquisitiveness, the willing subjection to the most monotonous and meaningless labor.

Emma tries to hide her anguish from Charles. He mentions that he has heard that Rodolphe is leaving and goes on to talk of what a "gay dog" the bachelor is. He offers one of Rodolphe's apricots to Emma, who falls back gasping. A moment later Rodolphe, on his way to Rouen, passes by in his blue buggy, and she screams and collapses on the floor. Homais revives her with aromatic vinegar, but she faints again, then falls into a kind of stupor. Charles and Homais sit up watching her, the pharmacist rambling on about nervous disorders and fits induced by odors; they assume Emma's attack was caused by the smell of apricots. Emma wakes briefly, shouting "The letter! The letter!" By midnight she has succumbed to "brain-fever." (An illness thought in the 19th century to be caused by severe mental shock.)

For forty-three days thereafter, Charles nurses her faithfully. Emma lies in bed, silent and apathetic. By the middle of October, she is well enough to sit up. "Charles shed tears when he saw her eating her first slice of bread and jam." A little later he is able to take her for a halting walk in the garden. She shuffles over dead leaves, smiling continuously, but then, when he urges her to rest on the arbor bench, where she and Rodolphe have made love so many times, she grows weak again. Her illness returns, but with other symptoms: pain in her heart, head and limbs, vomiting. Charles fears she may have cancer.

CHAPTER FOURTEEN

To add to the medical and household expenses incurred by Emma's illness, Lheureux takes advantage of the confusion by presenting a padded bill for the traveling equipment she had ordered. His manner is so overbearing that Charles, unable to resist but unable to pay, takes out a large loan at a steep rate of interest. At this time Lheureux is prospering in business deals all over the Yonville district. Charles worries about his debt, then reproaches himself for thinking about anything but Emma.

Comment

Charles' innocence and good nature tend to work against his own and Emma's best interests. Lheureux, a clever judge of character, profits from both husband and wife, playing one off against the other. The **theme** of his rise is counterpoised against the Bovarys' ruin. Indeed, he rises on the ruin of others.

As Emma slowly convalesces she shows an aversion to anything that might remind her of Rodolphe. She seems totally absorbed in her condition and the regular round of daily events. Each evening the priest, Bournisien, pays a visit. At the crisis of her illness Emma, in fear of death, had taken the sacrament and during that ceremony, half swooning, had had a vision of a celestial peace and purity surpassing all earthly love and joys. Now, in the dimming memory of that dream, she aspires toward humility and wishes to become a saint. She surrounds herself with rosaries and religious images. The cure, amazed by her fervor, writes to the Bishop's own bookdealer for "some work of note, for a female with brains," and receives a random assortment of high-toned Catholic manuals and fiction. Emma finds them annoyingly pedantic, absurdly untrue to life but reads them all.

The energy of her buried passion is now directed toward God, and "in the pride of her piety" Emma compares herself to noble ladies seen in paintings, who in magnificent gowns renounced the cruel world and went into retreat. She devotes herself to charity and welcomes the company of her upstanding mother-in-law and the ladies of Yonville. Justin, who chaperones the Homais children when they come to visit, has occasion to see Madame, forgetful of his presence, comb out her beautiful long dark hair, and is filled with love and awe. Emma regards him, as all else, with complete indifference. A strange combination of kind acts and a cold manner makes it impossible to distinguish where selflessness leaves off and selfishness begins in her. When spring comes and Emma feels stronger, her spiritual interests decline.

Comment

Once more Emma displays emotional opportunism. Religion can substitute, temporarily, for love because she can dissolve her identity in it as she does in a sexual embrace: "as if her soul, ascending to God, were about to be swallowed up in His love." Her religious phases follow a pattern, one of many, in her life.

Although to herself and to the other characters she seems to change, we are always made aware of her basic constancy of impulse.

As in the convent, her "spirituality" is mostly role-playing. The image of herself kissing an emerald-studded reliquary, kneeling before a Gothic prie-dieu feeds her vanity, and her desire to be a saint is in compensation for lack of worldly success. Flaubert gives this worked-up zeal a broadly comic treatment with such remarks as "She saw herself as possessed by the finest Catholic melancholy that ever ethereal soul could conceive."

When Emma is ill, thoughts of death remind her of God; when she is well she returns to more practical concerns. This transition from one phase to another is dealt with subtly. Rather than analyzing the decline of Emma's religious feeling, Flaubert gives us the scene of Justin admiring her beauty, and a scene with Felicite in which, after the maid has begged permission to go out (to meet her boyfriend), Emma moodily asks "Do you love him?" Thus we return to the erotic theme.

The cure continues to stop by, just to be sociable. In the evening he sits in the garden with Charles, Binet and Homais drinking cider, telling routine jokes. One day, when Homais suggests that Charles take Emma to the opera at Rouen, a discussion of the theatre's virtues and vices arises. Actually, the talk is, as usual, dominated by the pharmacist, who pretends to a scholarly knowledge and love of the arts. He especially enjoys baiting Bournisien who, not being very articulate, can only rejoin that "if the Church has condemned the playhouse, the Church has her reasons." Charles is persuaded that it would be good for Emma to have a treat and insists on the trip although Emma is reluctant.

Homais sees them off the next day, complimenting Emma's appearance: "What a hit you'll make in Rouen!" While Charles bumbles around the city, confused by the procedure of buying tickets, Emma purchases a new hat and gloves. Charles is so afraid of being late that they rush to the theatre without stopping for supper, and arrive before the doors are open.

Comment

The humorous tableau of the four provincials sipping cider and having an "intellectual" discussion provides a relief in tone from the frenzy of Emma's emotions and a picture of the absolute humdrum into which her life has fallen. At the same time it gently leads us into the story of Emma's second illicit affair through a dialogue on morality in which the champion of convention (Bournisien) is stifled. Ironically, prophetic, too, is Homais' parting compliment: "You'll make a hit in Rouen!" Once again Charles, unwittingly, leads his wife toward adultery.

CHAPTER FIFTEEN

When she sees the crowd milling around downstairs, Emma feels proud to have a box seat. Looking around her she sees merchants talking shop, and elegant young dandies striking poses in the stalls. A brilliant chandelier descends and the opera begins. A highland scene is represented and Emma finds herself back in the world of the novels of Sir Walter Scott. The music and costumes are thrilling; the scenery trembles when the actors cross the stage. To the accompaniment of a bird-like flute, Lucy, the heroine, sings her first aria. She is unhappy and longs to fly away with her love.

The famous tenor, Edgar Lagardy, appears. He is a handsome Mediterranean type, said to lead a life as romantic as the role he plays. Personal magnetism as well as a good voice have given him artistic fame. He is a charming mountebank who combines aspects of the "hairdresser and the toreador." When Lagardy and Lucy embrace despairingly, Emma recognizes all the tempestuous emotion she had known with Rodolphe, but he had never wept in the moonlight. The audience goes wild and the entire farewell scene is encored. Charles doesn't understand the plot. He confuses the hero with the villain, the real lover with the unloved fiancé. He says he likes to "get things straight" but Emma is too impatient to explain.

In the next scene sad Lucy is about to be married against her will. Emma wishes that she too had resisted, waited for the right man. Had she been able to combine the pleasures of love with marital fidelity how happy she would have been. But, alas, such bliss is impossible in real life! She is trying not to take the staged fantasy to heart when Lagardy appears in a black cloak, brandishing a sword, and Emma is once more enthralled. Ah, if chance had so ordained, she might have shared the amazing, glorious life of this man. They would have traveled everywhere, and during performances he would have addressed his impassioned songs to her alone. In fact, as the act ends, she imagines that he is looking at her and all but cries out, "Take me! Carry me away!"

During the intermission Charles pushes into the crowd to get his wife a cool drink, and after accidentally spilling most of it down the back of a Rouen lady, returns with the news that Leon is here. As the third act begins, Leon comes to the box, and from that point on the opera ceases to be of interest. Emma recalls all the sweet **episodes** of their unspoken love, wondering what strange fate has caused them to meet again. He is sitting so close behind her that she can feel his breath on her hair. "Does this stuff amuse you?" asks Leon, "Oh heavens, no," she replies. Leon suggests that they leave. Charles objects; he is just beginning to enjoy himself. But Emma insists that the mad scene is being overacted and Charles gives in.

At an outdoor cafe by the harbor they discuss Emma's illness, Leon's present apprenticeship with a business firm in Rouen, and the gossip of Yonville. Not much can be said in the presence of Charles. People who have just left the theatre go by singing, "Lucy, my beautiful angel," and Leon remarks that, compared to other opera stars he has heard, Lagardy is really second-rate. "All the same," says Charles, "I wish we had stayed." "Never mind," says the clerk, "he's giving another performance soon." The Bovarys had planned to leave the next morning but Charles suggests that Emma could stay on by herself. Seizing this unforeseen opportunity, Leon breaks into lavish praise of Lagardy's performance in the last act. Charles urges Emma to stay; he doesn't mind going home alone. "It's just," Emma falters with an odd smile, "that I'm not sure...."

Comment

Despite Mme. Bovary's recent religiosity, we find her more ready than ever to enjoy romantic illusions. The degree of her vulnerability may be measured by the extent to which she is carried away by Lagardy's charm, and the ease with which she resumes her relationship with Leon, despite the fact that he has been absent and virtually forgotten for three years.

The hammy opera, with its creaky scenery and flashy hero, provides an example of the extreme romantic style in art and, to some extent, a parody of Emma's life. We note that Emma does not stay to see the tragic ending.

MADAME BOVARY

PART 3, CHAPTERS 1 - 7

· ·

CHAPTER ONE

Leon, though still essentially timid, has gained experience and poise in Paris. He is no longer in awe of a mere country doctor's wife and resolves on a bold attempt to win Emma. They meet at her hotel the day after the opera and the old conversation resumes as if there had been no gap of three years, no Paris flirtations for Leon, no moonlit assignations for Emma. Creating idealized pictures of themselves, they prattle on about their aspirations, their sorrows, Emma's sickness, Leon's yearnings for the grave. Once, he mentions, he made a will requesting to be buried wrapped in the rug Emma made for him. "Why?" she asks. "Because I loved you."

Leon watches Emma's face grow radiant with his confession. She had always suspected it, she says, and their conversation shifts to reminiscences of their old days of joy and sorrow. Recollection and a growing sympathy enthrall them; they stare at each other "as though some vibrant message had passed between their gazing eyes." Leon remarks that he had often been frantic thinking of the happiness they might have had if they had met earlier. Emma, too, has thought this. "Why shouldn't we begin again?" he asks. But she tells him that she too old, he's too young; they should just remain friends. She repels his timorous caresses.

He begs her, at last, to meet him the next day-he has something "important" to tell her - and she consents, naming the Cathedral as rendezvous. As he leaves, he bends over the begins kissing the nape of her neck. "Oh, you're crazy, you're crazy!" she titters, but allows him to go no further. Later, Emma writes a letter cancelling their appointment, but realizing that she doesn't know Leon's address, decides to give the message to him herself.

Comment

Though the general bearing of Leon and Emma's conversation seems, at first, somber and melancholy, there is actually a strong undertone of excitement and desire. The comedy lies not only in the trite and affected things they are saying, but in their continual pains to hide their satisfaction, from themselves, from each other. Otherwise, Emma is much more brazen and unscrupulous than she used to be. It is she who makes the advances, just as much as Leon: alluding to her grief in such a way as to make clear she means grief of the "heart," encouraging him to talk about his love for her, permitting some physical liberties. It is not conscience now holding her back, as much as the desire not to sell herself too cheaply.

Leon is early for the appointment the following morning. It is a beautiful summer day and he carries a bouquet for the lady. He is dressed with all the care and elegance he can command. Avoiding the pompous old beadle, who is bent on giving a guided tour to every visitor, Leon slips into the Cathedral. As he walks around the shadowy and murmurous aisles, it seems that life has never been so good. Emma will soon be there. "The Cathedral was like a gigantic boudoir prepared for her." After a long wait, Emma appears-only to thrust her letter into his hand and disappear into one of the chapels.

As Leon waits impatiently, Emma tries to pray for resolution, but is only aware of the turmoil in her heart. She rises, and, encountering the beadle, welcomes the diversion of the tour. She and her chafing admirer go off on a circuit of the church, until Leon thrusts a coin into the beadle's hand and hurries her out. He orders a cab. She is hesitant: "You know it's not the thing." "It's done in Paris," he replies, and the word "Paris" decides her. As they huddle into the cab the beadle shouts from the Cathedral steps that at least they ought to have seen the reliefs of the "resurrection, the Last Judgement, the Paradise, King David, and the Damned in the Flames of Hell."

With drawn blinds, the cab jolts through the streets of Rouen. From time to time the baffled driver requests directions, but receives only the furious answer "Keep on!" Throughout the afternoon the citizens of Rouen are amazed by the spectacle of a cab appearing and reappearing at every corner, surmounted by a thirsty, desperate, almost weeping driver. Once, in the middle of the day, an ungloved hand emerges from beneath the blinds and drops a handful of torn paper-Emma's letter-which is carried off by the wind "like white butterflies." At six o'clock the cab at last comes to a halt, discharging a single passenger, a woman in a long veil who does not look back.

Comment

Frequently in old tales of courtly love, the lover first sees his beloved in church, in an aura of holiness and inaccessibility. An elaborate courtship ensues, in which, such is the lover's awe and the lady's purity, no physical union may be reached or even desired. The beginning of Emma's second affair, then, like her first, parodies a conventional situation. Where the virile Rodolphe was, appropriately, a knight on horseback carrying Emma away, Leon is the "poet" stunned by the encounter with his lady in church. This role is appropriate too, since Leon is a clerk, and a soft and "soulful" character. Further **irony** lies in the fact that this is not an accidental, but an arranged meeting, an assignation. Moreover, physical union is very much what Leon and Emma have in mind and what will be achieved almost immediately.

So completely have they perverted tradition that, rather than being spiritualized by their surrounding, they convert the church into "a gigantic boudoir." The old beadle leads them among the graves of the famous dead and reminds them of "King David" (an adulterer) and "The Damned in the Flames of Hell." For one moment his presence, "a heavy panting breath behind them, punctuated by the tap-tap of a stick," seems an embodiment of death or retribution, like the blind tramp Emma encounters later.

Emma's second seduction takes place not on horseback but in so plebeian an affair as a cab. Her imagination is no longer as fastidious as it was, evidently, and her lover is no longer a "gentleman" but a mere bourgeois. At the same time, the **episode** is an ironic parallel to her old day-dreams of a glorious journey (see Part One, Chapter Seven, and Part two, Chapter Twelve), though this is a city hack that jostles violently among the wagons and barrels of commercial thoroughfares, not a coach - and - four splendidly ascending the mountains. A sordid reality answers Emma's dreams - Flaubert emphasizing the actuality of the journey, as opposed to the vagueness of her imagined itineraries, by carefully listing all the streets in Rouen where the cab might be seen.

CHAPTER TWO

At the inn, Emma finds that she has missed the coach to Yonville, but by hiring a trap she manages to catch up with it. Felicite is waiting at Yonville to tell Emma that she must see Homais at once. The Homais family is busy with the annual preparation of jam, while its master is scolding Justin. The boy has dared to enter the pharmacist's laboratory, his "Capharnaum" (The reference is to Luke, 7; the town where Jesus heals the centurion's servant), in search of a pan. To impress Justin with the gravity of his profanation, Homais reminds him that arsenic is kept there in a little blue glass bottle labeled "Dangerous." Suppose the boy had touched it, then the pan? In his indignation Homais hardly notices Emma, but finally calms down enough to tell her that her father-in-law is dead. Out of regard for Emma's feelings, Charles asked the pharmacist to relay the "terrible" news.

Charles has been much affected by his father's death, though hardly fond of the old man. His mother, remembering only the good days, is grief-stricken. Emma, indifferent or absorbed in visions of Leon, finds her silence interpreted as sympathy. Actually, she sees Charles, even in bereavement, as weak, puny, "a cipher, a poor creature in every way," and cannot pity him. Lheureux comes by, ostensibly to have the doctor sign a new note. But, he tells Emma, with her husband's current worries it would be better if someone else could act for him: if she, for instance, could obtain Power of Attorney.

After the departure of her mother-in-law, Emma, coached by Lheureux, goes to work on Charles. She dazzles him with long strings of technical phrases, with such words as "order," "foresight," "the future." Finally, she shows him a document granting her Power of Attorney. But, she says, it has been made out by the town notary, whom she does not entirely trust. If only there were someone who could help! "Leon," suggests Charles. But it will be difficult to settle things by mail, and Charles is so busy. Graciously, Emma volunteers to go to Rouen for three days.

Comment

This chapter shows Emma becoming more deeply bound to Lheureux; more than his victim, she is now his co-conspirator. If her aversion for Charles has become less violent, settling down to mere contempt, she is prepared to treat him in a still more shabby and heartless way. We also learn in this section that Homais keeps arsenic on his premises, and that Justin has access to it: important facts for Emma.

CHAPTER THREE

The three days in Rouen are like a "real honeymoon" for Leon and Emma. They spend the day in their room in the Hotel de Boulogne on the quay beside the Seine. The blinds are drawn, and flowers strewn over the floor. At evening they cross the river to one of the islands, to dine in a low-ceilinged tavern with fishing-nets hung by the door. Afterwards, they lie on the grass under the trees and kiss. They wish they could live there forever, like Robinson Crusoe, in the little spot their love has made seem the most beautiful on earth.

One moonlit night as they are returning, Leon watches Emma in the stern of the boat, her slender form now shadowed by overhanging trees, now revealed "like a vision in the light of the moon." She sings an old song, "One night, do you remember, we were drifting . . ." He discovers on the deck a red silk ribbon, which the boatman identifies as being left by a recent party: "a lively lot of ladies and gentlemen" with cakes, champagne and hunting-horns. He recalls one of the group, a tall handsome fellow with a little moustache, a "real joker," a "regular lady-killer," whose name was "Adolphe . . . Rodolphe . . ." Emma shudders, blaming the night air.

When they part, Emma arranges for a secret correspondence using double envelopes, a device which Leon thinks very clever. He assures her that the papers granting her Power of Attorney are all right, but later, as he walks back alone, wonders why she was so anxious to obtain it.

Comment

The details make clear the fragile and unreal quality of Leon and Emma's affair. They hide from the day in their locked room, take refuge at evening far from the noise and activity of town. Their moonlit return, too, with Emma's nostalgic song dying away over the water, her form uncertain in the shifting light, suggests the impermanence of their happiness. At the same time, Flaubert emphasizes the commonplace character of their experience. The island they go to is no South Sea paradise, but an ordinary resort of pleasure-seekers, loose ladies and their companions - one of whom, recently, was probably Rodolphe. To an outsider, then, Emma and Leon would be just that: a loose lady and her gallant. We can see how certain elements of the reality she would deny will trouble Emma's peace: her past with Rodolphe and her machinations against Charles, which even disturb Leon.

CHAPTER FOUR

Completely absorbed by his first real affair, Leon snubs his friends and neglects his work. He lives for Emma's letters and finally, no longer able to endure her absence, journeys to Yonville. After prowling about the town and revisiting the Golden Lion, he calls on the Bovarys, but is unable to see Emma alone. They meet together briefly in the garden lane at night, in a driving rain. Death would be better than this terrible separation, Emma agrees, and she promises to find some way to see him regularly. They should be helped by some money she hopes to receive soon, and in that expectation she has already been indulging herself freely with Lheureux's wares.

Shortly afterwards, Emma begins to display a renewed interest in music, but her playing seems to have gotten quite bad. She needs lessons, but they're so expensive. She rejects a local teacher whom Charles proposes, but keeps on mooning over her piano while Homais tells the doctor it would be a crime to neglect his wife's talents, especially since Emma will be able to instruct Berthe, an ultimate saving. So Charles brings up the matter again and Emma persuades him to allow her to journey to Rouen once a week for "lessons." Flaubert remarks, "At the end of the first month she was thought to have made considerable progress."

CHAPTER FIVE

Every Thursday, Emma rises before Charles wakens and boards the Rouen coach, the "Hirondelle." She comes to know every inch of the way: fields, farms, outlying cottages, and, at last, the city with its river and islands, bridges and boulevards, under a pall of brown smoke. The spectacle of the town, the sense of manifold life and passions, fill her with excitement. Alighting near the city gates, she slips through obscure streets to the quarter of theaters, bars and brothels. Suddenly she sees Leon ahead of her; follows him to the hotel room. He opens the door. They embrace rapturously.

Life begins for them amid the garish, faded, "friendly" splendors of the Hotel de Boulogne. Between kisses, they pour out their accumulated store of endearments and anxieties. They feel as if the room were their home, playing the "eternal young-married-couple" at champagne-lunches before the fire. Leon tastes for the first time the "inexpressible delight of feminine elegance"; in her diverse moods Emma is the sum of all women he has read or dreamed about. They part crying "Till Thursday! Till Thursday!"

Occasionally on the trip back, the coach meets a ragged old blind tramp with a stick. He is a horrible sight, his eyelids "shredded into red ribbons," his face covered with green scabs. He sings a little song about birds and summertime: "When the sun shines warm above,/ It turns a maiden's thoughts to love." His voice sinks to the very depths of Emma's being, filling her with a "limitless melancholy." Sometimes he clings to the coach behind her until the driver whips him off.

Comment

The hollowness of the play-acted "honeymoon" is revealed by its setting. The hotel is in a disreputable district and its decor - the bed in the form of a cradle, the red hangings and soft carpets -suggests that it is a customary haunt of illicit passion. Moreover, the lovers' behavior shows cross-purposes and strains. Leon is fascinated by Emma as the "woman in love," as a "real mistress."

Once his curiosity and vanity are satisfied, he will not want her. Emma's anxieties and disappointments make her a kind of emotional "vampire," who would drain away all her lover's individuality. A typical scene shows Leon sitting at Emma's feet as she murmurs "Child, do you love me?" She would reduce him, if he let her, to infantile dependency.

The old tramp in his blindness and outward disfigurement embodies the inner corruption and ultimate ruin of Emma's life. He seems at once a type of Death or Doom and a kind of decayed, hideous Cupid presiding over diseased love. In his little song Flaubert says, in effect, "This is what it comes to, all this sentimentality and romantic **cliché**: it is the voice of corruption." Emma, it seems, half gets this message.

At home, Emma is first tired and strange with Charles. Her longing for Leon grows more desperate during the week, but she charms her husband with little attentions. Thursday's bliss comes 'round again, but she cannot expel a fear of losing Leon. She employs every device to wake his passion and jealousy, even telling him that she has loved before. A "ship's captain" he was, someone who will impress the clerk, but she swears that nothing "happened" between them.

One day a puzzled Charles returns home. He has just met Mademoiselle Lempereur, Emma's supposed music teacher, who says that she has never heard of Madame Bovary. She must have forgotten the name, says Emma. Or maybe there are several Lempereurs teaching piano in Rouen, suggests Charles. Emma makes a great search for the receipts for her lessons, until Charles begs her to desist. The next Friday he discovers the receipts in one of his boots, into which they must have "fallen." Subsequently, Emma has other scrapes. Father Bournisien, enquiring for her at her official stopping place in Rouen, The Red

Cross Inn, learns that she is seldom there. On another occasion, Lheureux meets her coming out of the Hotel de Boulogne with Leon.

Lheureux takes advantage of his discovery to put more pressure on Emma. He tells her he must have some money; instead of paying off Charles' notes, she has gone deeper into debt. When she says she has no money, the draper suggests that he find a buyer for a small property belonging to Charles. But when the money comes, yielding to Lheureux's persuasions, Emma keeps the cash and signs four new notes. She is sensible enough to pay off three, but the fourth arrives while she is in Rouen. Charles is stunned, Emma assures him, between caresses, that her purchases were cheap and necessary, that she just didn't want to bother him. Old Madame Bovary is called in to help and, though shown bills faked by Lheureux, is shocked by her daughter-in-law's extravagance and makes Charles promise to cancel the Power of Attorney. When Emma dramatically throws the document into the fire, Charles takes his wife's part and the old woman leaves. It takes much entreaty, later, before the offended Emma permits renewal of the Power of Attorney.

After this triumph she grows more "irritable, greedy, voluptuous." To Leon she seems wild, daring to walk openly with him in the streets of Rouen, but "adorable, magnificent." Sometimes, though, she dreads a meeting with Rodolphe, for she feels he still has some hold over her. One night she fails to return to Yonville, so Charles drives to Rouen. After searching all over, he meets her, by a lucky accident, on the street of Mademoiselle Lempereur. Emma tells him she was taken ill and that he is not to worry if she should stay overnight in the future. She begins to visit Leon whenever she feels like it, calling for him at his office. The clerk, though afraid of his employer's anger, embarrassed by Emma's dictatorial whims, is completely submissive to her. He has become "her mistress rather than she his." "Murmuring tender words, she kissed his soul away. Where could she have learnt that gift of corruption, so profound and well-dissembled . . .?"

Comment

The trap set by Lheureux is closing in on Emma. Meanwhile, we are aware of how her relationship with Leon contrasts with her affair with Rodolphe. Again, she is becoming more reckless, demanding and all-absorbed in her passion, as if to compensate for its shortcomings. But not it is now mainly her lover's unequal commitment which drives her, but her irritation over his lack of means and style and her general sense of entrapment. She would like Leon to dress in black and wear a beard, to have elegant rooms; perhaps unconsciously she is comparing him disadvantageously to Rodolphe. Furthermore, in this affair the roles are reversed: Emma is the "master," the corruptor, Leon the "mistress," the submissive one. In thus playing the "part" of Rodolphe. Emma may be inflicting a kind of revenge on the male sex (in the person of Leon) or indicating her continuing fascination for the virile, masterful Rodolphe.

CHAPTER SIX

One Thursday when Emma goes to the inn to catch the Hirondelle she finds M. Homais there. Leon had invited him to Rouen in return for the pharmacist's hospitality. Homais is very excited about the trip. Like Mme. Bovary, he is anxious to rise above provincialism. He uses Parisian slang and affects what he considers to be urbane manners. As soon as the coach reaches its destination, Homais drags Leon off to a fancy restaurant. While he revels in wine and unaccustomed luxuries, boring Leon with drunken discourses on women, Emma waits for her lover, wondering where he is, working herself up into a fury. After several hours Leon finally gets to the hotel. He is on his knees apologizing to the redeyed Emma when a servant announces that Monsieur is being paged. It is Homais again, who bullies the clerk into a new expedition. Fed up with waiting, Emmas leaves town before Leon gets a chance to return. Outraged by his apparent neglect, she considers all his faults: he is "incapable of heroism, weak, commonplace, effeminate, as well as parsimonious and chicken-hearted." Although she soon forgives him, her love for Leon remains tarnished.

Comment

That Emma finds it so easy to denigrate Leon proves that her love had a weak foundation to begin with. On the other hand, of course, her criticism of him is just. Basically, he is ordinary and weak. He is easily manipulated by those with stronger wills, even the tiresome Homais, who, as Flaubert points out more than once, parallels Emma in pretentiousness and petty tyrannizing.

Emma and Leon's meetings are never as wonderful as she expects them to be, but as if to compensate for his disappointment, Emma is more seductive and more possessive than ever. There is something "extreme, mysterious, mournful" about this desperate passion which begins to frighten Leon. The young man resents the woman's domination but is unable to resist her. One afternoon, after a rendezvous, Emma sits for a while in the arbor of her old convent. A stream of memories wells up . . . her youthful dreams, her honeymoon, the Viscount, Lagardy . . . and somehow her love for Leon seems as distant as all that has passed. She feels that she has never been happy. Promises of joy are always a deception. All is vanity. Yet passion is Emma's life.

Money problems, however, are forcing themselves to her attention. A stranger shows up one day with a bill which Lheureux had passed on to a banker, Vincart, at Rouen. Emma tells him that she will pay the next week, but the following day she receives a demand note stamped by the bailiff. Frightened, she runs to Lheureux and reminds him of his promise not to pass on her I.O.U.s. The draper claims that Vincart forced him to do it; he is not to blame. Both Monsieur and Madame Bovary owe him a great deal of money. He has tried to be helpful but right now he is unable to make further loans; he "hasn't a farthing." But he changes his tune when he learns that Emma still has money coming to her from her father-in-law's estate. A new loan is agreed upon "provided that Vincart will agree!"

Actually, as it turns out, the remainder of the legacy amounts to very little. Emma seeks new ways of raising money. She sends bills to Charles' patients without letting him know, sells her old clothes, borrows from everyone. Some money comes in but much more goes out; she falls further and further behind. The once meticulous Mme. Bovary now lets her household go to rack and ruin. Berthe is neglected, and Charles is afraid to complain. He is always fearful for his wife's health and attributes her ill-temper to a nervous ailment. Emma spends all day, "half-awake, half-dressed," alone in her room. Having managed to get Charles to sleep upstairs, she stays up all night reading blood-curdling stories, and yearning for "those rendezvous of which she had grown so weary."

Comment

Even Emma is aware that the underlying **theme** of her passion is decay: "Why did everything she leaned on instantaneously decay?" Yet, she tries to deny her disenchantment with excesses of the most fleeting pleasures, luxury and lasciviousness. Her inability to manage money is tied up with her general loss of contact with reality. Lheureux is comparable to a dope peddler who leads the addict into complete dependence and ultimate destruction, while giving in return a brief sense of happiness.

In this decadence everything begins to take on a sinister quality. As she tears off her clothing for Leon, Emma's laces go "whistling down over her hips like a slithering adder," the messenger from Vincart is grotesque, the garden is choked with weeds. Emma, lounging in her room, burning incense, titillating her inflamed imagination with gothic horrors, lives in a dream while her world collapses.

Only the days in Rouen count, and on them Emma spares no expense. Leon questions her extravagance and, when one day she asks him to pawn some silver spoons for her, he decides that his mistress is "getting into strange ways." Besides, people have been pressuring him to break off with her. Upon receiving an anonymous letter warning that her son was "ruining himself with a married woman," Leon's mother had written to his employer. Everyone knows. Reputation is important to Leon. He is about to become chief-clerk and is ready to renounce his former sentimental-esthetic enthusiasms. "Not a lawyer but carries within him the debris of a poet."

Leon is weary of Emma's tears, while she "has discovered in adultery all the banality of marriage." Their passion has been reduced to a degrading routine, but Emma cannot let go. Driving herself to regain the lost excitement, she writes love letters to Leon, imagining a fantastic lover who becomes more alive to her than any actual person. Emma is on the threshold of a nervous-breakdown. During Lent she stays overnight in Rouen and goes to a masked ball. All night, in a daring costume, she dances and carouses, but at dawn, finding herself in tawdry surroundings among students, clerks, and prostitutes, she feels sick and defiled.

That evening when she gets home a legal document is presented to her. If she cannot clear he debts within twenty-four hours all her furniture and belongings will be turned over to her creditors. Immediately she goes to Lheureux, but his manner toward her has changed. He is completely inflexible, cold, insulting; he even threatens to expose her to Charles. By the end of their interview she is tearfully begging him for just a few more days: "You drive me to desperation!" "That's too bad!" he says, as he shows her to the door.

Comment

Emma, the dreamer, wakes to find herself utterly abject and alone. Leon, having had his fling, has matured into a thoroughly bourgeois prig. Lheureux, having drained her dry, reveals his true nature. The masked ball which ends in a bitter dawn perfectly symbolizes this whole drama of illusion and reality.

CHAPTER SEVEN

The bailiff arrives next day to take inventory of the Bovarys' possessions. The sight of him fingering her belongings, even searching a box of Rodolphe's love letters for concealed money, fills Emma with fury. A guard is left, but hidden from Charles in the upper story, to secure the premises. Emma goes to Rouen to get help from the bankers. All refuse. Finally, she hurries to Leon's. She tells him of her plight. She must have money; he, Leon, can surely help. She will love him so. Helpless, frightened by her near hysteria, he hastens off, but returns empty-handed at the end of an hour. They sit for the last time in "their" room at the Hotel de Boulogne, staring at one another, silent. "I'd soon get it if I were in your place," says Emma. "Where from?" he asks. "Your office." There is such "diabolical recklessness" in her eyes, such willfulness and "sensual invitation," that he is afraid of yielding to her proposal. Promising another try for help, he leaves hurriedly.

She walks back to the Yonville coach, dazed and weeping, past the Cathedral where their affair began. Once she is almost run over by a carriage; she thinks she recognizes the driver as the Viscount from La Vaubyessard. She finds Homais aboard the "Hirondelle." Outside Rouen they encounter the blind tramp, and the pharmacist, though scandalized by his presence (he should be "shut up and forced to work") gives him a soul, with much moral admonition and medical advice. The imbecile beggar - after being told to keep out of bars, take "good wine, good beer, good roast meat" - goes into his "act," crouching in the dust, howling and rubbing his stomach. Emma throws him her last five francs: "it seemed glorious to fling it away like that."

Comment

It is a bitter wind-up for her affair with Leon. He is reluctant to receive her in his room because his landlord doesn't like his tenants entertaining "women," equating Emma with a casual pick-up. In their beloved hotel room they stare at each other across the empty fireplace. Instead of shared ecstasy, Emma feels only irritation at Leon's helplessness, Leon only fear of her lawless desperation. When he takes her hand on parting, he finds it "quite lifeless": everything has been drained away.

When Emma passes the Cathedral pouring out its Lenten Sunday crowd of the good bourgeois of Rouen, she sees the beadle, like a figure from his own Last Judgement, standing "firmer than a rock" amid the mob. While she is thinking of the day she met Leon there, she is almost knocked over by the gentleman in sables driving a black horse. This dark figure she identifies as the Viscount: appropriately since the ball at La Vaubyessard had such fatal consequences on her imagination. The final embodiment of retribution is the blind tramp, who howls like a "famished dog" outside the coach. She, too, is a "beggar" now, in spite of the reckless defiance of flinging away her last coin. But the wolfish appetite of Death or Corruption will not be satisfied by such a gesture; it demands Emma, body and soul.

The next morning at Yonville, Emma is awakened by a mob gathering around a signboard in the square: Justin is attempting to snatch down the notice of public auction. A weeping Felicite advises Emma to try the notary, Maitre Guillaumin, for she knows he is "interested" in Madame. The notary receives her at breakfast, in his dressing gown, a maroon velvet cap over his plastered-down thin hair. Emma admires the gleaming, middle-class opulence of his dining room: the sort she "ought to have." She tells him of her difficulties, with which, as a business associate of Lheureux, he is thoroughly familiar. She tries to appeal to his feelings, becoming deeply moved herself. He seems sympathetic. Why hasn't she come to him before, he asks, toying with her hand and whispering into her ear. She springs to her feet and asks for the money. Yet, he says, falling on his knees and grabbing her by the waist, only "... Stay! I love you!" Horrified and indignant, she runs out of the room.

She rushes home choking with a rage against all men that makes her want to strike out, trample them down. And with this, she feels a towering self-esteem, a gloating pride that Providence seems "bent on persecuting her." Back home her mood changes.

Charles will soon be there, and she cannot face the man she has betrayed and ruined, knowing that in the end he will forgive her: he, whom she could not forgive if he had a million. She is enraged by his superiority, cannot endure the "burden of his magnanimity." When she sees him coming through the gate, his face "as white as plaster," she runs out the other door.

Later, the mayor's wife sees Emma entering Binet's house. She and a crony find a window overlooking Binet's garret. He is at his lathe, turning out some useless knickknack with a smile of idiot absorption. Emma appears and begins some kind of appeal to Binet. They cannot hear her because of the lathe. Her manner is "tender, supplicating." The tax-collector looks on uncomprehendingly, then flushes and shouts "Madame! How can you think of such a thing!" Emma vanishes.

She takes refuge at the house of Mother Rollet, Berthe's old nurse. She lies in bed in a kind of stupor, losing herself in a flood of memories: the day she walked there with Leon, the glitter of the river, the smell of flowers ... Leon had promised to come that afternoon, so she sends the nurse to meet him. He will save her! Mother Rollet returns: nobody is around except Charles, weeping and calling for his wife. In a sudden flash, Emma thinks of Rodolphe. He, "so kind, so considerate, so generous," will help her. "... A single glance would remind him of their lost love." She sets off for La Huchette, "unaware she was hastening to expose herself to what a little while before had so enraged her, never for a moment suspecting prostitution."

Comment

Emma, who cherished such romantic illusions and was so exalted in her sentiments, is reduced to "selling" herself like a common prostitute. In the case of Guillaumin, it was he who did the propositioning, she who made the rejection, but with Binet she is the petitioner. Flaubert, by using the device of the "peeping Janes," leaves vague the exact nature of her "scandalous" proposal; thus, though it is almost certainly not of an erotic character, it can affect us as something equally shameful. In all this, there is one man to who Emma's pride will not let her go, the one man actually capable of understanding and generosity: Charles.

The idea of "prostitution" which runs through this chapter is not meant to enforce the doctrine that adultery, in the end, comes to nothing more than prostitution. This would be to distort Flaubert's intention. His moral indignation is directed rather at falsity than sexual transgressions, at the pretense and selfishness which often masquerade as love. Prostitution, an insincere and self-interested relationship, is a suitable analogy for Emma's affairs, and her punishment is that she must now face the real thing. Emma's love has always had to be "bought" - she paid herself with illusions, lies, Charles' money. In this respect, it is significant that her ruin comes in an economic form. Her vision of the "romantic" cannot exist without money; when the money goes, Flaubert seems to say, such bourgeois "false romanticism" goes too.

MADAME BOVARY

PART 3, CHAPTERS 8 - 10

. . . .

CHAPTER EIGHT

In the familiar environs of Rodolphe's house, Emma's heart swells with nostalgic tenderness. She walks down the dusty stone corridor to his room, hesitates for a moment, then enters. Rodolphe is astonished to see her, but quickly tells her she is "charming as ever," and accounts his desertion to motives upon whose secrecy the life of a third person depends. Overcome by his presence, Emma half believes him. She tells him how she loved him, how she suffered. Soon they are sitting with their fingers intertwined, as on the day of the Fair, and Emma is proposing that they start again. Rodolphe kisses her eyelids. He asks her why she has been crying. Emma bursts into sobs and Rodolphe kneels beside her, swearing he loves her and begging her to tell him what's wrong. "I'm ruined ...," she says, "You've got to lend me three thousand francs!" He rises to his feet, looking grave, as she pours forth a tale of embezzled fortunes, expected, legacies. "So that's it," thinks Rodolphe, growing pale. "I haven't got it my dear lady."

Emma loses control. All around her are luxurious ornaments convertible into cash. She would have given him everything, worked with her hands, begged in the streets! And, she would have been happy if she had never known him. Here, on this very place on the carpet, he vowed eternal love. For two years he led her through "the sweetest and most magnificent of dreams." Then he broke her heart with his letter. Now he turns her away because it may cost him three thousand francs! Rodolphe remains perfectly calm through this tirade: "I haven't got it."

She stumbles back through the estate, dazed by a rush of incongruous memories: her father, Lheureux, the room at Rouen . . . Strangely, she thinks no longer of her need for money, only of her martyred love and her humiliation. At one moment the air seems filled with little globes of light; in the center of each is the face of Rodolphe. Then she recognizes them as the lights of Yonville shining through the trees. A sudden resolution comes to her, "a transport of heroism which almost made her gay," and she runs down the path to Homais' pharmacy.

Comment

In this **episode** the sincerity of Emma's emotions is ambiguous. Certainty her reconciliation with Rodolphe is convenient and amazingly rapid, though we know that he has remained, in a sense, the man in her life. Her final speech of denunciation is crucial. When she claims that she would have sacrificed everything for him, have labored, begged, we recall that much of Rodolphe's fascination for her lay in the wealth and luxury he represented. Moreover, Emma has been so greedy of pleasure, so incapable of material sacrifice. Nevertheless, allowing for such contradictions and all her exaggerations and literary turns of speech, her words have a ring of sincerity, even a certain nobility-as if, seeing Rodolphe's selfishness so clearly now, she also saw the real possibilities in her own nature for devotion and sacrifice.

Justin is alone in the shop. He sees Emma's white face outside the window. She seems "extraordinarily beautiful, possessed of a ghostly majesty." He lets her in, and in a low "sweet and melting" voice she cries "I want it! Give it me!" Seizing the key to Homais' laboratory, she opens the door and grabs a blue jar from the shelf. Before the terrified Justin can interfere, she has crammed her mouth full of the white powder. "Don't say anything!" she hisses, and then walks away, "suddenly at peace."

Charles, confronted with abrupt and total ruin, has spent the day searching for Emma. He finds her, at last, at home writing a letter. She tells him to ask no questions, but read it tomorrow: now she must lie down. She falls asleep, and wakes with an acrid "inky" taste in her mouth, begs Charles to give her a glass of water. Suddenly she vomits; an icy coldness begins rising from her feet. Charles notices a whitish sediment in the basin. It's nothing, she says, but begins to groan loudly and is seized with convulsions. Charles implores her to tell him what she has eaten, looking at her "with such tenderness in his eyes as she had never seen before." Finally, she lets him open the letter. He reads a few lines and begins crying "Poisoned! Poisoned!"

Felicite fetches Homais Messengers are despatched for Canivet, the surgeon who amputated Hippolyte's leg, and Dr. Lariviere, Charles' old teacher at Rouen. Frantically Charles searches through his medical dictionary: he does not know what to do. Emma begs him not to cry. "It had to be my dear," she says. Charles beseeches her: "Weren't you happy? . . . I did all I could." "Yes," she says, "You are a good man." His grief is redoubled by this unprecedented tribute-to lose her at such a moment!

At last Emma feels herself beyond all the squalor and lies. She calls for Berthe, and the little girl, thinking from all the lights it is some holiday, keeps asking for her "gift." She is frightened by her mother and has to be taken away. Canivet arrives and prescribes an emetic, but soon Emma's condition get worse. She begins vomiting blood, her limbs writhe, she breaks into horrible screams, begging the poison to be quick. Dr. Lariviere enters and with one glance knows Emma is doomed.

Lariviere leaves, telling Charles he will be back; there is nothing he can do. Homais begs the distinguished physician to have luncheon with him. After elaborate preparations they sit down, and the pharmacist entertains the great man with a parade of his erudition. The Homais children are brought down to receive the doctor's opinion of their constitutions, while have the rest of town: Mayor Tuvache, Binet, Lheureux, Madame Lefrancois, gather in the pharmacy for a free consultation. Lariviere pushes through them and rides off.

Father Bournisien appears in the square carrying the crucifix and holy oils. When Emma sees the priest her face lights with sudden rapture, as if experiencing the joy of her old mysticism. Bournisien presents the crucifix. "Reaching forward like one in thirst, she glued her lips to the body of the Man-God and laid upon it with all her failing strength the most mighty kiss of love she had ever given." The priest begins to anoint her body: the covetous eyes, the false and lustful lips, the hands so eager to caress, the feet that ran so swiftly toward desire . . .

Her face wears a look of serenity, and Charles feels new hope. Suddenly, as if waking from a dream, Emma calls for a mirror. She looks in it for a while, then big tears begin to run down her cheeks. With a sigh, she falls back on the pillow. The death agony begins: her chest heaves, her tongue protrudes from her mouth, her eyes roll in her head. Suddenly, above the rattle of her breath, Charles' sobs, and the priest's Latin, rises the sound of clumping shoes, the scrape of a stick, a hoarse voice singing "When the sun shines warm above,/ It turns a maiden's thoughts to love." Emma sits bolt upright. "All across the furrows brown/ See Nanette go up and down,/ Gathering up with careful hand/ The golden harvest from the land." "The blind man!" Emma screams. And she begins laughing horribly, "fancying she could see the hideous face of the beggar rising up like a nightmare amid the eternal darkness." A last convulsion throws her back upon the mattress. "The wind it blew so hard one day,/ Her little petticoat flew away!" Emma is dead.

Comment

The sentimental literature of Emma's day was full of lover's suicides, beautiful and touching deaths. At the height of the romantic movement suicide was a "fashion" among melancholy young men, who tried to emulate their heroes from Goethe or Vigny. Emma, too, aspires to such a glorious death; it is her ultimate romantic delusion. We see her attempting, in turn, to be stoical, serenely mysterious, forgiving, affectionate, religious: to display sentiments which will ornament her death-bed and prove her, after all her failures, a true romantic heroine. But none of it works. She has not reckoned with the horrible reality of death-a reality of which Flaubert gives a prolonged and most gruesomely clinical account.

In her last moments Emma is true to form in other ways. The kiss she gives to the effigy of Christ seems more the expression of her invincible sensuality than of any religious impulse. It is like a climactic kiss given to a lover; her last, unfailing lover. Once again she will be disappointed, however, for the image she carries to her death is the beggar's hideous face. The presence she must meet on the other side is not her Saviour, but the embodied nightmare of corruption.

At the end of the chapter we hear more words of the blind tramp's song. The coy and silly lyrics jar horribly with Emma's death, robbing it of its last dignity. Moreover, the song is one of the popular **ballads** in which the lyrics have a conventional sexual meaning: the blowing of the "wind," the loss of the "little petticoat" stand for deflowerment or sexual intercourse. This is an appropriate meaning to bear on Emma but, beyond this, in the context the words have a more sinister significance, suggesting the "wind" of death, the loss of flesh and its vanities.

CHAPTER NINE

When he sees Emma lying so still, Charles throws himself upon her crying, "Goodbye! Goodbye!" Homais and Canivet drag him from the room. The pharmacist leaves for his own house, meeting the blind man in the square; he has come to Yonville for some medicine Homais recommended to him. After spreading the story that Emma mistook arsenic for sugar while making vanilla cream, Homais returns to the Bovarys.

He finds Charles in a kind of stupor, sitting downstairs. The pharmacist reminds him that he must arrange for the funeral. Charles stammers, "No! I want to keep her." Finally Father Bournisien arrives and manages to persuade Charles to write his instructions for the funeral: Emma is to be buried in her wedding-dress, wearing a wreath, with "her hair spread out over her shoulders"; and three coffins, one oak, one mahogany, one lead; and a piece of green velvet over all. The priest and the pharmacist are astonished by Bovary's romantic and expensive notions. Bournisien takes him out in the garden and attempts to reconcile him to the will of God, but Charles shouts, "I hate your God!" He stands for a while in the rain, watching the passengers of the "Hirondele" alighting one by one.

Homais and Bournisien undertake to watch the dead woman, relieving the monotony by disputing on the truth of religion and the efficacy of prayer. Charles enters to look at Emma. Already her body is beginning to change. Her mouth hangs open and her eyes are clouding; the sheet sinking into the declivities of her body seems pressed down by an enormous weight. Charles leaves, and the argument of the two watchers breaks out more acrimoniously: "Read Voltaire! Read the Encyclopedia! . . . Read the Proof of Christianity!" Charles returns. He has thought of catalepsy, wonders whether Emma might be brought back to life if he willed it strongly enough. "Emma! Emma!" he cries.

Comment

Under the strain of his loss, Charles' character begins to change. In his grief he becomes "romantic": struggling against separation from his wife, insisting she be buried like a bride, blaspheming against God. We find, too, a new stubbornness in him. His refusal to alter the funeral plans persists, we shall see, even when his mother condemns them. Above all, the sincerity of his love is evident in every action.

Old Madame Bovary arrives. Charles kisses her, bursting into tears, but becomes furious when she objects to the cost of the funeral. More visitors appear, to show their good breeding in hours of boredom before the fire. In the evening Homais returns, bringing aromatic herbs and chlorine water to sweeten the air. Felicite and Madame Lefrancois are dressing the body.

The landlady remarks on Emma's unaltered beauty, but as they raise her head to put on the wreath, a stream of black liquid pours from her mouth, like vomit.

Bournisien and Homais resume their dialogue. Mention of Charles' husbandly suffering leads to the questions of the celibacy of the priesthood and the effectiveness of confession. Homais falls asleep and the priest wakes him by opening a window. They hear a dog howling in the distance. Homais drops off again, and Bournisien soon follows suit. They sit opposite each other, "bellies protruding, faces puffed and scowling," united in sleep, stirring no more than the corpse. Charles comes in. Emma seems to him to be disappearing under the moonbeam whiteness of her dress and veil, to be melting into the quiet night. He remembers her, vital and beautiful, at Tostes, in Rouen, at Les Bertaux. A "terrible curiosity" grips him. Slowly and apprehensively he raises her veil ... and shrieks with horror.

Charles is taken downstairs by the awakened watchers. He asks for a lock of Emma's hair, which Homais supplies; he trembles so that he punctures the skin and leaves white patches in her hair. Through the rest of the night priest and pharmacist keep their watch: falling asleep, waking to blame the other for falling asleep, alternately sprinkling holy water and chlorine around the room. In the morning Felicite brings in bread, cheese and brandy, and the two fall upon it ravenously, chuckling together from time to time, until Bournisien smacks Homais' shoulder and declares, "We'll get along fine before we're finished!"

Emma is nailed into her coffin: the sound of the hammers is torture to Charles. Then the coffin is carried downstairs to be enclosed in the outer two. The doors are opened for the people of Yonville. Emma's father, old Rouault, arrives and seeing black cloth hanging from the house, faints away in the square.

Comment

A major emphasis of this chapter-carrying further the physical horror of Chapter Eight-is Emma's swift dissolution. This is brought out not only by such details as the clouding eyes, the dark liquid, Charles' scream of horror, but is felt in the very atmosphere of the room, where the smell of death seems to grow more intense with every application of aromatics or chlorine. Emma's dream of a romantic death is not to be supported even to the extent of allowing her a beautiful corpse.

This monstrous joke of a Fate which seems determined not to leave her a shred of dignity is exaggerated by the clownishness of her watchers. Neither of them have any real feeling for Emma. They alternate between asinine bickering and brutish slumber: the dead watching the dead. The world of Yonville, somnolent and empty, must surround Emma to the last, even inflicting a final violation as Homais ravages her beautiful hair. In the end, Yonville science and religion chortle happily over their morning brandy, ready to put romance in the grave.

CHAPTER TEN

The letter to Rouault from Homais had been worded so discreetly that Emma's father was not sure whether she was alive or dead. As soon as he had recovered from the initial shock, he had mounted his horse and set off at a gallop. At dawn he saw three black hens in a tree and took them for an evil omen, but later it seemed to him that the countryside could not look so peaceful, the sky so blue if Emma were dead. Alternately his hopes rose and fell. Sometimes, in his great anguish, he hallucinated: heard voices, saw an image of Emma's corpse lying on the road. By the time he rode into Yonville, the flanks of his horse were covered with blood.

He recovers consciousness in Bovary's arms and weeping asks what had happened to Emma. "I don't know, I don't know, it's a curse that's on us," Charles sobs. Homais urges them to be "brave, philosophical." Soon the ceremony begins. Bells toll, choristers chant, the harmonium groans, the priest intones in a shrill voice. Charles has an impulse to blow out the candles by the bier. Though he tries to find faith, to believe they will meet in the afterlife, the knowledge that she is about to be covered by the earth fills him with rage and despair. Hippolyte, wearing his best leg, is seen awkwardly kneeling in the aisle. A collection plate is passed around; "Be quick! This is terrible for me!" hisses Bovary. The rites go on and on, then the bell starts tolling again. As the congregation files out of the church, a pale Justin comes out of the pharmacy for a moment, and quickly withdraws again.

The funeral procession proceeds through the town, past curious crowds, and out through fields and trees. The heavy odors of wax and cassocks mingle with the fresh scents of flowers and grain; the solemn De Profundis is accompanied by the distant rattle of a cart, a cock crowing. Charles recalls how on other such spring mornings he visited patients on this route and then went home to Emma. As the pall-bearers near the cemetery, they tire and the coffin "moves forward in a series of jerks like a boat tossing at every wave."

Finally the coffin is lowered into its plot. When Charles' turn comes to sprinkle holy water on the grave, he cries out "Goodbye," throws kisses, and knee-deep in earth "drags himself to the edge that he might be swallowed up with her." When it is all over even Charles and Rouault feel relieved. Homais takes note of various improprieties such as Rouault smoking his pipe, Binet being absent, the lawyer's man wearing blue rather than black. No one expresses more grief than Lheureux: "Such a good woman! To think that I saw her in my shop only last Saturday!" Homais regrets that he hadn't time to prepare a funeral oration.

Charles, Rouault, and Mme. Bovary Sr. sit in mournful silence at home. Rouault recalls how he consoled Charles when his first wife died and comments that now there is nothing left for him. He has lost his wife and children. He will return to Les Bertaux that evening; he can't bear to stay in this house. He looks back once as he leaves Yonville, just as he had turned to watch Emma ride off after her wedding. The setting sun is reflected in the windows of the village. He goes slowly for his horse is lame.

Charles' mother plans to stay and keep house for her son. She tactfully hides her delight at the prospect of regaining his affection. When the midnight bells ring, Charles is still awake, thinking of her. Rodolphe in his mansion, and Leon far away, are sleeping peacefully. But at Emma's grave Justin is weeping. Lestiboudois sees the boy as he runs away and believes that he has found the person who has been stealing his potatoes.

Comment

Aside from the obvious point of the hypocrisy of Lheureux and Homais, this chapter is notable for its mocking similarity to the wedding scene. A ceremonious procession winds through streets and fields. Emma, now in her coffin, wears her wedding dress again. But the lovely spring weather, rather than seeming to participate in the joy of the occasion, merely reminds us of nature's indifference to human events. Where once a fiddler led the way, now a choir chants the De Profundis. In a sense the funeral is the ultimate outcome of the marriage. As for romance, the only true mourners for Emma are her simple-hearted husband and a young boy, the lovers to whom she was always completely indifferent.

CHAPTER ELEVEN

Berthe is brought home and soon begins to forget her mother. Charles' creditors seize the opportunity to harass him: not only Lheureux, but others like Mademoiselle Lempereur, who charges Charles for three month's music lessons. To make things worse, he refuses to part with any of his wife's belongings, while he soon discovers that Emma had secretly collected for most of his outstanding bills. Sometimes, Felicite wears a dress of Emma's and seeing her from behind, Charles will cry, "Stay! Stay there!" A few months later she elopes, carrying off Emma's wardrobe. About the same time, Charles receives notice of Leon's marriage to a Mademoiselle Leboeuf. He thinks of how pleased Emma would have been.

One day, poking through the attic, he finds a ball of crumpled paper, a letter. He reads, "Be brave, Emma, be brave!" It is Rodolphe's farewell. Charles recalls his strange behavior at the time, his sudden disappearance. But perhaps, he tells himself, it was a "platonic love between them." It was natural for everyone to adore Emma. And the thought of her allure fills him with a terrible and unappeasable desire. As if she were still alive, he begins to conform to her tastes, wearing patent-leather boots and white cravats, waxing his moustache - and signing promissory notes. "She was corrupting him from beyond the grave."

He sells the silver, the furniture, everything but the furnishings of Emma's bedroom. Little Berthe runs around in ragged clothing, though her pretty ways delight Charles who mends her toys and plays with her. The Homais children, following papa's instructions, have ignored the child since her father's social decline.

As Charles' fortunes ebb, Homais' are rising. The blind man has taken to telling everyone of the failure of the pharmacist's ointment for his eyes. Homais fills the Rouen paper with squibs denouncing the tramp as a public nuisance and succeeds in getting him committed to an institution. Elated by success, he becomes the self-appointed spokesman of progress and anti-clericalism, aspiring to still more illustrious roles. He compiles a Statistical Survey of the Canton of Yonville, with Climatological Observations, ventures into philosophy, problems of morality and commerce. While not neglecting his pharmacy and pushing all the latest medical fads, he adopts the "artistic" manner, even taking up smoking.

Charles and Homais visit Rouen to buy Emma's tombstone. The pharmacist has proposed a draped, broken column, or a pyramid, a Temple of Vesta, but settles for the choice of the memorial inscription. Charles thinks continually of Emma, though he is distressed to find her image fading. Every night he has the same dream: he is just about to embrace her when she crumbles to dust in his arms. Meanwhile, his debts grow heavier. He quarrels with his mother, who would have helped him: once because he refuses to give her a shawl of Emma's, again because he is unable to go through with plans to let her take Berthe. His attachment for the child has grown as he loses all other ties.

Comment

Though Emma is dead, her presence continues to dominate the book, torturing and "corrupting" Charles. His financial plight and the hostility of his mother continue to worsen.

He cooperates with his ruin, turning his life into a morbidly "romantic" celebration of her memory, refusing to face the truth about her. Meanwhile, as if Emma's death had removed some mysterious barrier or Charles' ruin provided some mysterious incentive, Homais sprints toward success.

Homais begins a campaign for the Legion of Honor. His claims are numerous: his "devotion to duty at the time of the cholera"; his membership in "several learned societies" (he belongs to one); his publication of *Cider,* its Manufacture and Operation and other works; his service with the fire brigade. The ardent, progressive, child of the Revolution, begins to court the Establishment, secretly aiding the Perfect in the election, writing an adulatory petition to the king. A little plot in his garden is shaped like the star of the Legion, with two strips of grass for ribbons.

One day, after deferring it for weeks, Charles opens the secret drawer in Emma's writing desk. Leon's letters are there ... "No doubt this time!" In a sobbing frenzy, he ransacks every corner of the house, at last finding the box with Rodolphe's portrait and love-letters. The discovery utterly desolates him. He never leaves the house, not even for patients. The rumor spreads that he has taken to drink, and a few who spy into the garden see him pacing back and forth, sloppy, unshaven, weeping continuously. Only in the evenings he takes Berthe to visit her mother's grave or visits Madame Lefrancois just to talk about Emma.

One day when Charles is in a neighboring town to sell his horse, he meets Rodolphe. Both grow pale, but Rodolphe quickly recovers and invites Charles to have a drink with him in the tavern. Charles stares with envy at this man whom Emma had loved; it is as if "he were looking at something of her." Rodolphe chatters about crops and cattle, dreading an **allusion** to Emma, and carefully watching Bovary's changing expression. At one point he is even frightened by a look of "sombre fury" on Charles' face, but "the old look of dismal lifelessness" returns. "I'm not angry with you," Charles says. Then, "with a resigned accent of infinite sorrow," adds the "one large utterance" of his life: "It was the fault of Fate." Rodolphe thinks him "rather comic ... and a bit abject."

The next day Charles sits in his garden. It is clear and warm, the air filled with the scent of jasmine and the sound of bees. Charles feels suffocated by the "vague currents of love that swelled his stricken heart." In the evening Berthe comes out to summon him to dinner. He is leaning against the wall, his eyes shut, with a lock of black hair in his hand. Berthe calls to him, and thinking he is playing a game, gives him a push. He topples to the ground, dead.

The autopsy ordered by Homais can discover no organic cause of Bovary's death. The sale of the last of his possessions raises just enough money to send Berthe to her grandmother. But the old lady dies within the year. Since Rouault is paralyzed, the child is sent to an aunt, who being poor has Berthe work in a cotton mill. After Charles, three doctors follow one another in Yonville, but none of them can make a go of it, so great is the prestige of Homais' treatments. "His practice grows like wildfire. Authority respects and public opinion protects him. He has just received the Legion of Honor."

Comment

Emma's final blow to Charles-the revelation of her infidelity-is not enough to kill his love, though ultimately it kills him. Has he managed to purge his love of all resentment and self-interest, or is it that a long habit of adoration and the persistence of her vaguer, idealized image prove too much for him? He seems to have risen to a comprehensive, if simple, philosophical view of things: "It was the fault of Fate." Rodolphe, who has always used the word as a synonym for his own appetites, finds it comical - and it is. For Charles probably got the idea from Rodolphe's letter and it ignores the role of so many people and concrete circumstances: Emma, Leon, Charles himself, Yonville, the times. Nevertheless, it may be a generous and even adequate pronouncement, forged in suffering and an honest attempt to face his life's incomprehensible tragedy. In the end, too, it is Charles-the boy with the ridiculous cap at Rouen, the bourgeois clod, the cuckold-who dies the "romantic" death: a broken-hearted victim of "Fate" with a lock of beloved hair in his hand.

Afterwards, while his little Berthe goes to work in the mills, Homais, the irrepressible mediocrity, receives his Legion of Honor. That award, conceived in the heyday of Napoleonic romanticism to honor heroism, learning, art, and public service, now goes to a banal and vulgar time-server. Whatever our individual judgements of Emma and Charles, whatever her corruption, his stupidity, it is clear that the ruin of the Bovarys and the rise of Homais symbolize the destruction of a spiritual potential, and the triumph of something utterly gross and soulless.

MADAME BOVARY

. . . .

Emma Bovary

A beautiful young woman whose frustrated search of ecstatic love, glory and refinement in a dull provincial environment provides the plot of the novel. She is the type Flaubert classified as the "false" romantic: emotional but not warm-hearted; sentimental rather than artistic; sensual rather than spiritual. She places all importance on appearances rather than inner values. To some extent her illusions and affectations, as well as her more serious faults, deceit and selfishness, are due to external influences such as the prevailing romantic decadence in art, and the bad luck of marrying an insensitive, earth-bound bourgeois, of loving men who cannot understand her, and living in unattractive, deadening small towns. Ultimately, she is as much the victim of a grossly materialistic society as of her own deluded romantic notions.

Flaubert's attitude toward her is ambiguous. Generally, he treats her with **irony** and contempt. On the other hand, she reflects certain romantic tendencies of his own which cause him, and the reader, to be somewhat sympathetic.

Charles Bovary

A provincial health-officer and husband of Emma. As his name (Bovary) suggests, this character has much of the "bovine" or cow about him. He is rather ridiculous, stolid, unambitious, ordinary, naive, unemotional. Charles is easily manipulated by other people: his mother, his first wife, Emma, Homais. He asserts himself against others only for love of Emma, his second wife, whom he adores. Even when she is unfaithful to him and ruins him financially, he forgives her and continues to worship her. When she dies he assumes some of Emma's romantic manner, orders green velvet to be draped upon her coffin and attempts to dress elegantly. Unable to live without her and continually brooding over her memory, he dies of a broken heart.

We both laugh at and pity him, but, in the end, he provokes some admiration, for through the worst experiences he remains profoundly innocent, good-natured, honest and loyal. His story, rather than Emma's, opens and closes the novel, enclosing it, as it were, in a framework of banality.

Rodolphe Boulanger

Emma's first lover, the gentleman proprietor of La Huchette, an estate near Yonville. A good-looking, self-confident and virile man of thirty-four, Rodolphe seems the "white-plumed cavalier" of Emma's girlish dreams. Actually, he is a shrewd, hard-hearted and unscrupulous libertine, who takes her up as a diversion. As country gentry, Rodolphe belongs to a class which has largely ceased to have any functions or interests other than hunting, the mastery of horseflesh and easy women. Shallow and opportunistic himself, he cannot recognize the sincerity behind Emma's often-heard words of love. She becomes inconvenient and tiresome, and after corrupting and exploiting her to the limit, he cynically abandons her.

Leon Dupuis

Emma's second lover, first a law clerk in Yonville, later apprentice to a businessman in Rouen. Leon contrasts with Rodolphe, being timid, inexperienced, passive, and rather feminine. If Rodolphe is the dark cavalier, Leon-a mere bourgeois clerk-is the fair, blue-eyed "poet" of Emma's life: at least she makes him write poems to her. He and Emma are drawn together by their common romanticism, and their love affair has a determinedly "romantic," willfully rapturous quality. Essentially, however, Leon is a timid and conventional bourgeois. He is dominated and corrupted by Emma - in their relationship, he is the "mistress" - but soon becomes resentful and frightened. Like Rodolphe, he forsakes Emma when she needs him, and soon after her death marries a Mademoiselle Leocadie Leboeuf. Her last name, meaning "ox" or, figuratively, "bumpkin," suggests the bovine respectability to which Leon ultimately allies himself.

Homais

The pharmacist of Yonville, Homais is the type of "secular intelligence" in the provinces. A degenerate heir of the great rationalist tradition of the 18th century, he is the mouthpiece of the most banal and superficial ideas of the age. As an amateur chemist and meteorologist, he is inaccurate and trivial. His "enlightened" anti-clericalism is as safe and dogmatic as the piety he attacks. Though ostensibly an adherent of the principles of the French Revolution, he does not hesitate to support and flatter the monarchy. The quality of his mind is clearly revealed in the style of his articles for the Rouen Beacon: florid, affectedly poetic, self-propagandizing, false. A quack of all trades, Homais' activities are solely motivated by a hunger for self-advancement and a ridiculous vanity. His success at the end of *Madame Bovary* symbolizes the triumph of falseness and mediocrity in 19th century France.

Father Bournisien

The red-faced, athletic cure of Yonville, who epitomizes the failures of the provincial clergy: Homais' religious counterpart. A hard-working, well-intentioned man, a great help in harvest time and dutiful pastor to his flock, Bournisien is so unimaginative and materialistic that he cannot recognize the profounder spiritual needs and problems of an Emma Bovary. The Christianity he teaches his parishioners is a matter of form an a few simple moral precepts, without the higher meanings of his faith. He and Homais preside over Emma's deathbed like vultures of anti-romantic mediocrity.

Binet

Yonville's tax-collector and captain of the fire brigade, a former soldier. Binet, as the stiffest and shallowest figure in the novel, a kind of cardboard automation, represents the spirit of Yonville in all its vacuity and dullness. Binet is a man of few words and fewer interests; his main avocation reveals the man; the turning out of hundreds of wooden napkin-rings on his lathe. Aside from an occasional foray at poaching, this hobby-the manufacture of "holes" - consumes all his spare time, and, since he never gives his napkin-rings away, the activity symbolizes the acquisitiveness, the willing subjection to meaningless labor, of the Yonville bourgeois. At the crises of Emma's life, after Rodolphe's letter and before her suicide, the hum of Binet's lathe rises like the song of a demented Siren.

Lheureux

The draper and money-lender in Yonville, Lheureux completes the quartet of bourgeois infamy in *Madame Bovary*. Homais represents provincial science and learning; Bournisien, religion; Binet, officialdom; Lheureux, business and finance. His name means the "happy" or "fortunate one," and he is as triumphantly successful as Homais. Dark, bowed, insinuating and obsequious of manner, Lheureux is Emma's personal "devil." Like the traditional Tempter, he preys upon his victims' vanity, love of luxury, guilt, and distraction, and derives as much satisfaction from their humiliation and ruin as the material profits that accrue to him. In the end, his treatment of Emma is openly sadistic and gloating, though he counterfeits distress at her death.

Rouault

Emma's father, a good-natured and self-indulgent farmer. Sentimental, like his daughter, and so devoted to good living that he must keep selling off his property, Rouault is still a likeable man, unpretentious and kindly. He has not only given Emma some of her qualities, but has provided her with an education unsuited to her social position. In his occasional appearances and in his letter, he brings into Emma's world something genuine and warm, which even she is responsive to.

Madame Bovary Senior

Charles' mother, by the time of his marriage to Emma a pious, severe and rather dictatorial woman. Her character has been formed by the years of suffering and humiliation she has endured with Charles' father. His brutal disregard of her feelings, his repeated infidelities, embittered her and made her shift all her affection to her only son, whom she spoils and dominates. She resents and distrusts the daughter-in-law who has supplanted her.

Charles Bovary Senior

Charles' father, a former assistant-surgeon-major, forced to resign from the army because of some fraud. After catching a well-dowered wife on the strength of his good looks, Bovary Senior retired to the country for a life of liquor and lechery. Vain, brash, inconsiderate, he fancies himself as a fee-thinker and man of the world. He has never given a thought to his wife's feelings, and shows little care and affection for his son.

Justin

Homais' nephew and rather harassed apprentice, a boy of about sixteen. Aside from Charles, Justin is the only one in Yonville who genuinely loves Emma and sincerely mourns her death. It is he who gives her the key to Homais' laboratory, where she obtains poison. After her death, he runs away to Rouen to become a grocer's apprentice.

MADAME BOVARY

Question: What is Flaubert's attitude toward Emma Bovary?

Answer: Critical opinion on this matter ranges from those who find Emma thoroughly shallow and contemptible to those who regard her as a sympathetic and tragic figure. Some have even accused Flaubert of being "unfair" to Emma-the ultimate tribute to her vitality and independence as a character.

The best clue, perhaps, to Flaubert's feelings about Emma is his famous statement, "Madame Bovary, c'est moi": "I am Madame Bovary." Notwithstanding his attempt to suppress outward signs of identification, Flaubert deeply with his heroine, and if his treatment of he seems so ambiguous, it reflects the ambiguity of his feelings about his own romanticism. Undoubtedly, he cast off on Emma all that seemed most vicious or foolish in the romantic code. She becomes a scapegoat for the sins of the romantic tribe. However, one sometimes is made to feel that Emma is more sinned against than sinning.

Although Flaubert underplays them, she has some notable romantic and middle-class virtues. She tries to "improve" and educate herself, to add beauty and significance to her life, although it is true that these efforts are misguided and short-lived. At least once, in her final scene with Rodolphe, she reaches a certain nobility and sincerity. Although Flaubert has violated his rule of impersonality to remind us that "it was necessary for her to derive a sort of personal profit from things," we may sometimes feel that Emma's real faults were as much the limitations of her intelligence and bad luck as hard-heartedness or calculating sentimentality. If she had only a drop of the artist's critical detachment, if she had married anyone else but Charles, she might have been a better woman.

It is when Emma becomes a sufferer that **satire** must lapse. While it is true that her last visit to Rodolphe, for instance, has the most dubious motives, that even in her suicide there is something shabby and false, in both cases her agony is genuine. And Flaubert, though he might have preferred otherwise, could not entirely withdraw his sympathy from a sufferer even when she had "only herself to blame." Emma remains an embodiment of failings to which we all, Flaubert included, are liable. Above all, she receives a punishment for these faults which is so cruel and unusual, at once so disproportionate and poetically just, that we almost feel she is being sacrificed in a kind of vicarious atonement for Flaubert's and our own romantic crimes. We cannot despise such a victim.

Question: What is Flaubert's attitude toward Charles Bovary?

Answer: Like Emma, Charles has been a much debated character. He has been dismissed as an "utter clod" and extolled as "the only genuine romantic in the novel." It would seem that both positions have an element of truth, and that both are wrong.

Charles is, first of all, the principal factor in Emma's tragedy. It may be objected that if she had been more clear-sighted and warmhearted, Emma would have seen what a "good fellow" Charles was and settled down to happy domesticity. But this is being unrealistic and unfair to Emma. "Good-fellowship" in the Bovary sense is an extremely limited thing. Intelligence, understanding, imagination, interest, sensitivity are as important human values as good nature, and Charles lacks them. Certainly, many of Emma's objections to him are frivolous, but basically he is an impossible husband for her.

Charles, though, is more than mere "Charbovari," the boy with the funny hat that represents all the vulgarity and stupidity of his age. Flaubert cannot fail to grant some respect to anyone who works hard and does a good, useful job. Charles is hardly a brilliant physician, but most of the time (except for the disastrous clubfoot **episode**) he knows his own limits and works diligently within them. He is vastly more useful to society than the playboy Rodolphe or the law-clerk Leon. Moreover, Charles undergoes some interesting changes during the book. Out of his genuine love for Emma and his loss of her, he becomes something of a romantic, more sensitive, "deep," and original. Not only are the feelings that inspire this changes touching and creditable, but there is an element of the noble as well as the ridiculous in his new manner.

Flaubert, however, calls Charles' belated romanticism "corruption:" a kind of posthumous infection from Emma. And probably nobility, heartbreak, romanticism, form an atmosphere particularly unsuited to Charles: as we see, it ultimately chokes him to death. If he had only married an uncomplicated peasant girl interested in cooking, children and money in the bank, there would have been little question of his being a decent and useful man. To make anything more of him (as Emma tried) is as much an injury as to make anything less.

Question: What is Flaubert's view of romanticism in *Madame Bovary*?

Answer: The defects of romanticism were of two kinds: those which had participated in its spirit even at best, and those which infected it when it became a fashion. Belonging to the first group are the tendencies toward exaggerated individualism, perceptual vagueness, intellectual confusion, emotional extravagance, moral ambiguousness: the vices, in short, which both science and classicism opposed. The Flaubert also objected to them is implied by the qualities of his style, which is lucid, disciplined, temperate, detached, precise. At the same time, his interest in day-dream and revery, the subtleties of individual psychology and mood, the meticulous depiction of nature, and his use of symbolism, suggestion and indirection show him to be a romantic writer.

As for the imported vices of fashionable romanticism, criticism of these is the explicit subject of *Madame Bovary*. What had happened to romanticism is what happens to any movement when it becomes fashionable. People took it up who were really incapable of understanding it, for whom it was not a challenge to feel more vividly, think more clearly, live more earnestly. It became vulgarized, sentimental and banal, a way of hiding reality and distorting feeling. Above all, it degenerated into the **cliché**. Illustrative of this is the entry under SEA in Flaubert's compilation of clichés, the Dictionary of Accepted Ideas: "SEA: It is 'bottomless.' Image of the infinite. Inspires sublime thoughts." These are virtually the same things that Emma and Leon, that a thousand Emmas and Leons, said of the sea at their first meeting.

For these sins of fashionable romanticism Flaubert has no sympathy, though he has some for the heroine who commits them. A basic movement of the plot of *Madame Bovary* counterposes the fall of the Bovarys to the rise of Homais and Lheureux. The latter represent an extreme of banality, self-interest and materialism beside which, at their darkest, Emma's sins are only gray. Romanticism at least presupposes a certain generosity of spirit, a certain intellectual or emotional endowment-even the fashionable or "false" romantic may have these, but they are entirely lacking in such hard-headed careerists and acquisitors as Homais and Lheureux.

Question: To what extent does *Madame Bovary* exhibit the "impersonality" or "impassivity" which Flaubert regarded as primary quality of good fictional style?

Answer: Generally, compared to his predecessors, Flaubert succeeds remarkably well in keeping himself out of the book. The long passages of analysis or moral reflection common to earlier novels are absent. Insofar as possible, Flaubert has substituted for them devices which make analysis and comment "objective"; such, for instance, would be the description of an external scene to render the mood or thought-process of a character, or the famous **episodes** of "double action" like the scene at the fair, where one strand of action provides a commentary on the other without the author's intervention. Above all, whereas most writers perpetually call on the reader to identify with their **protagonist**, to adopt his viewpoint, share his ambitions, suffer his wrongs, Flaubert does not permit this. In fact by subtle shifts of tone and perspective, he keeps pushing us away from Emma.

It has already been suggested, however, that Flaubert was not really impassive" in the book. For instance, although when dealing with Homais or Lheureux, Flaubert never says explicitly, this is a fool, this is a scoundrel, we have no doubt of his contempt and indignation. **Irony**, the classic device in which a writer says "nothing" or says other than he means, is not impersonal. The writer who uses it is not really letting facts speak for themselves, but calling attention to an underlying or opposing meaning. Thus, there is not a word that Homais can say where Flaubert doesn't make the implicit comment: this man is a jackass. Moreover, the book is not devoid of more explicit moral commentary. To say of Emma, "she had little loving-kindness and was not readily susceptible to other people's emotions," is to so grossly violate the rule of impersonality that we may even want to question the statement's truth. Finally, there is with Emma, both on Flaubert's part and ours, an irrepressible element of identification. Most of us are sufficiently like her and sufficiently self-critical that we not only recognize and sympathize with her aspirations toward the splendors of love, fame, luxury, and travel, but identify with her very failures.

Question: Identify and illustrate some of the typical technical devices employed by Flaubert.

Answer: (1) The rendering of mood or thought-process by the description of external events or scenes. This is illustrated in Emmas' first disillusionment in Part One, Chapter Seven; her walk with Leon in Part Two, Chapter Three; her feelings after the seduction in Part Two, Chapter Nine; her near suicide in Part Two, Chapter Thirteen; and her "honeymoon" with Leon in Part Three, Chapter Three. (See the relevant sections in the Chapter Outline.)

(2) The use of symbols. Examples would include Emma's repeated dreams of travel and their ironic parallels (the Hirondelle, the cab in which she begins her affair with Leon), symbols of the romantic vision and the answering reality; such

figures of doom as the blind tramp and the beadle; the Viscount and his cigar case as symbols of romanticized aristocracy; Binet's lathe as symbolic of Yonville monotony; and the color blue as symbolic of happiness.

(3) The use of repetition. The three "loves" of Emma's life (Charles included) follow the same pattern: their beginnings in illusion, the later attempts to disguise the shortcomings and intensify passion, the final disillusionment. She has many other recurrent phases or moods: her periods of religious enthusiasm, of nostalgia for innocence, remorse, indifference, physical illness, etc.

(4) The use of contrasting **episode** or scene. Such is Emma's wedding opposed to the La Vaubyessard ball; her visions of travel in a carriage opposed to her seduction in a cab; the ball at La Vaubyessard and the masked ball in Rouen.

(5) The use of "double" or simultaneous action. Such are Emma's first conversation with Leon, carried on against the conversation of Homais and Charles; the country fair scene, with Rodolphe's blandishments undercut by the orations below; the amputation of Hippolyte's leg, which forms a background to the opposed thoughts of Emma and Charles; and the scene at the opera, where Emma's thoughts counterpoint the action on stage.

(6) The use of the **cliché**. Almost everything Homais says of a "scientific," anti-clerical, or "liberal" nature is **cliché**. Emma's youthful dreams and early conversations with Leon are tissues of romantic cliché. Rodolphe's "line" and letter are composed of seducer's clichés. The speech of the prefect's deputy is an example of bureaucratic or political **cliché**. The art of using these comprises the initial recognition of the **cliché** (Flaubert recognizes more expressions as **cliché** than would the ordinary

man), placing them among other appropriate **clichés** to bring out their banality, and using them in such a way that they advance the action, reveal character and undercurrents of motive.

(7) The use of types and anti-types. Emma herself, individual as she is, is a type of the false romantic. Charles, at least initially, is the unromantic bourgeois clod: Emma's anti-type. Homais is the type of the provincial "scientist" and free thinker; Bournisien his anti-type, the provincial priest. Leon and Rodolphe are opposed types: the bourgeois false romantic and the aristocratic libertine.

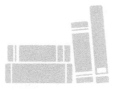

THREE TALES

A SIMPLE HEART

. . . .

SECTION ONE

A Simple Heart opens with a picture of the maid, Felicite, and the Aubain household sometime around Felicite's sixty-eighth year. For half a century the women of Pont-l'Eveque have envied Mme. Aubain for her servant, a model of loyalty and efficiency who can wash, sew, iron, cook, fatten chickens, and make butter to perfection. Mme. Aubain had been left a widow with two young children and a small income, and had retired to Pont-l'Eveque some fifty years ago. Her house is described in detail, from the wainscotted parlor with such obligatory bourgeois adornments as a piano, barometer, marble fireplace and ornamental clock, to Felicite's room on the top floor. Every morning Felicite comes down before mass, works uninterruptedly all day, then falls asleep before the fire with rosary in hand. A stubborn bargainer, fanatically clean, grudging herself food, she is thin and sharp-voiced. In all seasons she wears the same drab costume, and from the age of twenty-five has looked like a middle-aged woman.

Comment

Flaubert begins by presenting us with the cardinal fact about Felicite: hers has been a life of selfless labor which has seemingly reduced her to a kind of automaton. This can best be realized retrospectively, by looking back on her fifty years of service, and as against the background of the redundant, if rather meager, middle-class vanities of the Aubain house: the clock like "a temple of Vesta," the sheet-covered furniture of the salon, the unread books of the study. The "facts" about Felicite are only external, however, as emphasized by such phrases as "people took her to be forty," "she showed no age at all," "she seemed like a woman made of wood, performing like an automaton."

SECTION TWO

The story is taken up during Felicite's girlhood. An orphan at an early age, she was left in the care of a farmer, who put her out in the fields to tend cattle, neglected and beat her. But later, "like any other," Felicite had her "love story." When she was eighteen, she met a young farmer Theodore at a country fair. He treated her to refreshments and a silk scarf, then took her out into a field and tried to push her to the ground. Several days later she encountered him again on the road at evening. He apologized for his behavior, blaming it on drink, and began to talk about local affairs. He mentioned that his family wanted him to settle down, and asked her whether she had ever thought of marriage. She accused him of making fun of her, but putting his arm around her waist, he swore he was serious. They walked down the dusty starlit road together behind a huge hay-wagon drawn by four horses. He kissed her and she ran off into the darkness.

Soon they began meeting regularly. Felicite was no innocent, having been raised among animals, but resisted Theodore's advances until he promised to marry her. Shortly after their affair began, he confessed that he was afraid of military conscription. After torturing her for weeks with this, he told her that he would visit the local prefecture for information and meet her afterwards. At the rendezvous, Felicite found one of Theodore's friends, who told her that her lover had married a rich old woman to avoid the draft; she would never see him again. She threw herself on the ground, weeping and calling on God until morning. At the end of the month, she left the farm and soon settled in Pont-l'Eveque with Mme. Aubain.

Comment

The most effective disproof of Felicite's "woodenness" is evidence that she loved and suffered for someone. At the same time, we see early instances of the pattern of exploitation that Felicite will suffer from all her life. Throughout these passages dealing with Felicite's relatively "rich" early life, we retain the image of her as a dried-up old woman of seventy.

During her first months with Mme. Aubain, Felicite is amazed by the "tone" of the household and enraptured by Madame's children, Paul and Virginie, ages seven and four (named after the **protagonists** of a famous sentimental novel of young love). She soon becomes happy in the routine of the house. Every Thursday, friends of the Madame arrive promptly at eight for cards and leave before eleven. On Monday comes the bustle and noise of market, with visits from the tenants of Mme. Aubain's two little farms. Sometimes the Madame's uncle, the impoverished and dissipated Marquis of Gremanville, arrives; to be ushered out by Felicite when he has had too much to drink and begins telling risqué stories. Her special favorite is the imposing Monsieur Bourais, a retired lawyer who manages the Aubain properties. He has given the children a geography book with pictures of cannibals in feathered headdresses, a monkey carrying off a girl, a whale being harpooned. Paul's explanations of these illustrations constitute Felicite's entire literary and geographical education.

Often the family goes for excursions to a nearby farm of Mme. Aubain. While the Madame sits mournfully in a ruined country house, the children play in the fields. One misty evening while they are returning across the meadows, they are frightened by cows, but Felicite, stroking one animal's back, reassures them. In the next field, however, they encounter a bull. Felicite tears up clods and begins throwing them at the bull's eyes, covering the escape of Mme. Aubain and the children and narrowly missing being gored. Though the **episode** is talked of in Pont-l'Eveque for years, she never considers she has done anything heroic.

After this fright, Virginie develops a nervous disorder and sea bathing at Trouville is prescribed. The family sets out on horseback, stopping for luncheon at the other of Mme. Aubain's farms, a picturesque but ruinous place. At Trouville Virginie begins to improve. There are daily outings to the hills beyond town where the sea can be seen sparkling under a blue sky, or trips to the beach at low tide to collect starfish. Their chief amusement is watching the ships return: the slow gliding with lowered sail, the dropping of the anchor, the men coming in with baskets of fish to their waiting wives.

One day one of these women identifies herself to Felicite as her sister. She is married, with three children whom Felicite dotes upon and provides with shirts and blankets, though Mme. Aubain resents the way the family "takes advantage" of her servant. Finally, since the weather is bad and Paul must be sent away to school, the Madame decides to return to Pont-l'Eveque. Felicite will miss the boy, but finds a consoling interest in Virginie's approaching first communion.

Comment

Several important **themes** are brought forward in this section. One is the suggested decline of the genteel Aubain family, a background against which Felicite's loyalty is all the more salient: the visits of the disreputable old Marquis of Gremanville, Mme. Aubain's moonings in the ruined country house, the stop at the old farm with its mushrooms, mistletoe, fallen apple trees, and mouldering thatch. A second is the parallel of Felicite's with a saint's life. We see her first in St. Francis-like communion with the cows to whom she murmurs "a sort of lament." Then, like St. George of the dragon, she saves the family from the bull. Felicite is always close to animals, sharing their simplicity, inarticulateness and victimization; here, however, they may have other symbolic implications. The cows are patient, serviceable creatures like Felicite; the bull is an embodiment of the passion she will subdue in herself.

Though talking to cows and taming a wild bull are auspicious early "miracles" in the legend of Ste. Felicite, this is her youthful period of secular happiness. However commonplace the family's little trips, they make this the most exciting and varied time of Felicite's life. The scenes at Trouville, where Flaubert spent his summers as a child, are particularly evocative and full because of the brilliant selection of detail and use of **imagery** appealing to several senses at once.

Every day Felicite accompanies Virginie to catechism class, listening while the priest outlines biblical history, weeping as she hears of the crucifixion of the good and humble Jesus. The Gospels speak in pastoral images familiar to her and sanctify the common things of life. "She loved lambs more tenderly out of love for the Lamb, and doves because of the Holy Ghost." But she cannot understand Church dogmas and finds it difficult to imagine the Holy Ghost-is He bird of flame or breath? She enters into the devotions and feasts of the Church and her religious feelings reach a climax during Virginie's first communion. Anxiously, she watches the little girls in white parading up to the altar, and when Virginie opens her mouth to receive the Host, Felicite almost swoons. The next day she herself takes communion, devoutly, but without the same rapture.

Comment

With the explicit introduction of religion into *A Simple Heart,* we observe two things about Felicite. First, as a very simple person, her imagination tends to work on a literal level: symbols are invariably confused with reality, lambs with the mystic Lamb, doves with the Holy Ghost. Second, it is typical that her strongest feelings should be vicarious or sympathetic, not immediate. She almost faints when Virginie, with whom she lovingly identifies, receives communion, but her direct experience is weaker.

Mme. Aubain decides to send Virginie to a convent to complete her education. The girl's parting upsets her mother, but she is consoled by correspondence and other distractions. Felicite's grief is so keen that she cannot sleep or work properly, and at last she is permitted to send for her sister's eldest son, Victor. The boy comes every Sunday after mass, lunches with Felicite, then accompanies her to vespers. She mends his clothing and gives his family gifts and money. When the Aubain children return for vacations, Felicite finds they have grown away from her, so Victor is her only consolation. He is maturing into a good-looking young man who brings her souvenirs from his trips as cabin boy to England and the Channel ports.

One day Victor tells her that he has signed on for a voyage to America which may last for two years. The thought of his long absence dismays Felicite, and on the day of his departure she walks twelve miles to Honfleur to see him off. She loses her way in town, but finally reaches the harbor; there to think that she is losing her mind for suddenly she sees "horses in the heavens . . . ." A crane is lifting the horses into a boat. She spies Victor leaning against a rail but the gangplank is raised before she can get to him. The boat is towed away from the wharf by singing women and she watches it until it disappears on the moonlit sea. Afterwards she stands weeping and praying for a long time before the town's stone Calvary.

In the following months she worries continually about Victor, imagining him storm-tossed or dying of thirst, being eaten by cannibals or carried off by apes as in Paul's geography book. When Mme. Aubain is impatient because she had has no mail from Virginie in four days, Felicite reminds her that she hasn't heard from her nephew in six months. "Oh, your nephew!" her mistress replies and Felicite is hurt by her brusqueness. Soon she forgives her, however: it seems so natural to dote on the delicate girl. On one occasion, learning that Victor's boat is in Havana-a place she imagines as full of tobacco smoke-she delights Bourais, the lawyer, by asking him to point out "Victor's house" on the map.

Two weeks later a messenger arrives with a letter for Felicite from Trouville. Mme. Aubain opens and reads it: Victor is dead.

Overcome with grief, Felicite falls back in a chair. Mme. Aubain and the messenger leave, while Felicite thinks, "They don't care! It means nothing to them!" She rises mechanically and goes down to the river: she must do the washing. "The heavy beating she gave her laundry could be heard in the nearby gardens . . . while deep down (in the river) tall weeds swayed, like the hair of corpses floating in the water." In her room that night she breaks down completely. Long afterwards she learns that Victor died of yellow fever and bleedings, the doctor remarking as he died, "There! another one!"

Comment

Often, to "make" a saint, God will systematically deprive him of every earthly prop and comfort. Thus, the Aubain children grow away from Felicite and Victor dies. His parting, particularly, with its apparitional horses and singing women suggests a supernaturally destined end. Opposed to Felicite's grief is the callousness of Mme. Aubain and the doctor. For a moment Felicite even feels resentful, but her typical gesture is to submerge herself in labor.

Felicite's affections now center on Virginie, whose delicate health has broken and now shows signs of consumption. The girl regains a little strength in the autumn, but one day, returning from an errand, Felicite finds Mme. Aubain hurrying to depart for the convent. She rushes to the church to light a candle, then runs for an hour after the carriage. Just as she catches up to it, she remembers that she left the house unlocked and must return. The next day she takes the coach to the convent and arrives in time to hear Virginie's death knell.

For two nights Felicite sits up with the girl's body, praying over it, dressing it for burial, cutting off a lock of long blonde hair. At the burial she suffers a double grief: it is as though Victor were being interred with Virginie. In the weeks that follow she tends Virginie's grave daily and does her best to comfort the apathetic Mme. Aubain. Finally, she reminds the latter that she must take care of herself "for the sake of her son, and in remembrance of 'her.'" "Her?" replies Mme. Aubain, "as though she were emerging from sleep."

Comment

Virginie's death, paralleling that of Victor, is the second great blow to Felicite. We see here, incidentally, how the time of travel, once suggestive of richness and joy, has come only to mean bereavement: instead of the idyllic excursions to Trouville and the farm, Victor goes to America, Virginie to the convent to die. One event in this **episode** is typical of Flaubert's ambiguousness. We know that Felicite would give anything to be with Virginie before she dies, but after running so long to catch the carriage, she leaves to lock up the house. Is this self-sacrificial allegiance to duty or a ridiculous and pathetic bondage to habit?

The years after Virginie's death are marked only by the recurring feasts of the Church, minor household incidents, and the deaths of old acquaintances. One night the driver of the mail coach announces the July Revolution (1830, fall of the Bourbon monarchy), and shortly afterwards a new subprefect is appointed, a former consul in America who has a Negro servant and a parrot. But such events mean less than letters from Paul, who is breaking his mother's heart by refusing to take up a profession and contracting tavern debts. The two women console themselves by talking constantly of Virginie. One lovely summer day they decide to examine the girl's belongings. They spread out on her bed the girl's petticoats, stockings, handkerchiefs, a little moth-eaten plush hat which Felicite begs as a memento. The two women gaze at each other with tear-filled eyes, and for the first time in her life, Mme. Aubain takes Felicite into her arms. "They held each other close, assuaging their grief in a kiss that made them equal." Afterwards, Felicite cherishes Mme. Aubain with "a devotion that was almost animal and with an almost religious veneration."

The kindness of Felicite's nature grows. She comes to the door with cider for the passing soldiers, tends cholera patients, protects the Polish refugees. Especially, she takes care of a broken-down old man named Papa Colmiche, who lives in a pig sty near the river. She supplies him with linens, cleans out his shack, and when a tumor "the size of his head" bursts on his arm, she dresses it daily. When he dies she has a mass said for him.

On the day of Papa Colmiche's mass, "fortune smiles" on Felicite. The subprefect's servant arrives with the parrot as a gift for Mme. Aubain. The bird, associated with America and Victor, had fascinated Felicite and she had remarked that Madame would love to have him. The subprefect is moving to a new post and takes this way of disposing of the bird.

Comment

Flaubert gives us a vivid sense of a life in which the whitewashing of the vestibule in 1827 is as important as the overthrow of a king. Against this background Felicite's "saintliness" grows, even including the traditional tending of the "leper" in the person of old Colmiche. As often in the legends of saints, too, this particular act of charity has an immediate reward: the gift of the parrot.

SECTION FOUR

The parrot is called Loulou. His body is green, his wing-tips pink, his forehead blue, and his throat golden. Mme. Aubain finds him a nuisance, dirty and raucous, and gives him to Felicite. The bird is soon trained to say 'Nice boy" and "Hello, Mary" but remains obstinately silent with strangers, who hurt Felicite by calling him a "turkey" or "log of wood." He is fond of company, though, growing excited during Madame's Thursday card parties and deriving much amusement from M. Bourais, who comes to hate and shun the bird. Eventually, Loulou is given run of the house, though Felicite worries about his maneuvers going up and downstairs and about his enmity to Fabu, the butcher's boy. Once she cures a growth under Loulou's tongue by scratching it off with her fingernail; another time, while she is sunning him in the yard, he disappears. She searches madly all over town, and finally, when she returns heartbroken, the parrot drops from the sky onto her shoulder.

Felicite never recovers from this fright. As a result of a cold and ear infection, she loses her hearing. The pealing of church bells, the lowing of cattle, all sounds are lost to her except the voice of Loulou. With his imitations of the fish-vendor's cry, the carpenter's saw. Mme. Aubain, he recreates a world for her, and the two hold long and completely sincere-on Felicite's side-conversations. "Loulou was almost a son and lover to her in her isolated world."

One winter morning, Felicite finds Loulou dead in his cage. He has died of a "congestion," though she suspects Fabu of poisoning. She weeps so much that Mme. Aubain suggests that she have Loulou stuffed. Arrangements are made with a taxidermist, and Felicite decides to take the bird as far as Honfleur herself. On the road a mail coach comes up behind her. Felicite cannot hear the shouts of the driver nor can he stop the swift-moving coach. The horses graze her and the furious driver lashes out at her with his heavy whip, knocking her into the road. When Felicite recovers consciousness, before wiping the blood off her face, she makes sure that Loulou is all right. She sits by the roadside, eating a crust of bread and gazing at the bird for consolation. Finally at Honfleur, seeing the lights of the town, a wave of memories of her childhood, her first love, Victor, Virginie, comes flooding over her.

Comment

We should not say flatly that Loulou is the "Holy Ghost," come to reward Felicite for the years of devotion culminating in her goodness to Papa Colmiche. However, we can see how Loulou, in the pattern of his relationship to Felicite, resembles the divine spirit. First, he is the most beautiful and exotic thing she has ever seen, and the only such thing that has ever really belonged to her. He is silent with strangers, only speaking to the "good" (Felicite) and, similarly, "sees through" Bourais, who has but the semblance of goodness. He mysteriously disappears once, as the divine spirit sometimes forsakes the godly, then unexpectedly drops out of the sky. In communion with him, Felicite "loses" the world (through her deafness), but the bird replaces it with a new world, becoming everything to her. For him, finally, Felicite suffers a physical "martyrdom": she is scourged on the roadside by the driver of the mail coach. It is the world's parting blow, for with this and her last upsurge of memory and grief at Honfleur, one feels that Felicite has virtually reached the end of her pilgrimage.

It is so long before Loulou arrives that Felicite begins to fear he has been stolen. Finally, he returns, magnificent on a branch set in a mahogany base, biting a gilded nut. He is put in Felicite's bizarre little chapel of a room among her other treasures: rosaries, medallions, statues of the Virgin, Victor's gifts, Virginie's plush hat. Loulou stands on a shelf near the window where Felicite can see him in the first light and think of the "old days."

Her life sinks into a kind of "trance," broken only by the excitement of Corpus Christi day (the Catholic feast honoring the Eucharist). In church she always gazes at the stained glass window depicting the Holy Ghost, noticing its resemblance to a parrot, and buys a religious picture representing the Holy Ghost with purple wings and an emerald body. The Father must have revealed himself in a parrot, she thinks, because doves cannot talk.

A great event occurs: Paul's marriage. At the age of thirty-six, he has finally settled down and found a vocation, that of registrar, and is marrying his chief's daughter. Shortly afterwards, news comes of Bourais' death by suicide. Checking her accounts, Mme. Aubain finds the lawyer had long been cheating her, and her distress weakens her so that she contracts pneumonia and dies. Felicite mourns her bitterly, feeling it unnatural that her mistress dies before her.

Left alone with a small annuity, she retires more deeply into herself. She makes a special cult of the Holy Ghost, praying before Loulou's shelf in her room and going into "ecstasy" whenever a ray of light flashes from his glass eye. Because she is afraid of eviction, she never complains about the condition of the house, and after a cold and damp winter, she contracts pneumonia. "Ah! like Madame," she thinks, hearing the diagnosis.

Corpus Christi is approaching and Felicite has nothing to give to adorn the altar. To her great joy, the cure permits her to give Loulou. She grows weaker and sends for Fabu to apologize for her suspicions about his poisoning the parrot. The woman tending her brings her Loulou for a last farewell. The bird is beginning to disintegrate, one wing is broken and his stuffing is coming out. But Felicite is blind now. She kisses the bird and presses him against her cheek.

Comment

Again, Felicite's behavior is ambiguous. Is her cult of the dead bird a kind of absurd idolatry or does it represent, since now there is nothing to be gotten from him, the purest form of love? In any event, we see the complete fusion in her imagination between the Holy Ghost and Loulou, and she makes the ultimate sacrifice of her life by giving him up.

SECTION FIVE

Felicite wakes to the sound of bells. As if she were there, she sees the procession: the firemen, the choir, little girls scattering rose petals, the deacon, the cure under a red canopy. The murmur of the crowd rises, falls; there is a rattle of gunfire in salute of the monstrance. "Is he all right?" Felicite asks, thinking of the parrot. Her death agony begins as the sound of instruments and the voices of men and children mount upward. Her nurse glances down at the altar. It is hung with green wreaths and lace, decorated with relics, candlesticks, vases of flowers: in the midst of a bunch of roses Loulou's blue forehead is visible, like "a piece of lapis lazuli."

The priest ascends to the altar. The crowd kneels. The blue smoke of the censers rises upward. Felicite inhales it deeply, with a mystical sensuousness," then closes her eyes. "Her lips were smiling. The beating of her heart became fainter and fainter, softer like an exhausted fountain, like a fading echo; and when she breathed her last breath, she thought she saw in the opening heavens a gigantic parrot, hovering above her head."

Comment

The final ambiguity: is it mere delusion or has God, accepting a simple faith, chosen to appear to Felicite in the form most comprehensible and beloved by her? To answer this question, one might have to undo the marvelous union of affection and **irony**, lyricism and **realism** which form the story. Perhaps, moreover, the life of the most authenticated saint is not without such ambiguities as Felicite's. At least, Flaubert would think that any devotee must ultimately "take the chance" that his god is only a figment of his imagination, a projection of his longing. The one certain thing is the respect and affection that Flaubert has for such a "simple heart."

THREE TALES

THE LEGEND OF ST. JULIAN THE HOSPITALLER

. . . .

SECTION ONE

Julian's father is lord of country in which there has been peace for many years. A just and noble man, he lives with his pious, beautiful wife in a medieval castle complete in every detail: with moat and towers, garden and arbors, chapel and barns. The castle overflows with the accumulated goods of peace: tapestries and linens, casks of wine and bags of gold, piles of unused weapons in the armory. After many prayers, a son is born to them, and a great feast is celebrated to honor the event. Julian's mother is alone in her room when an old hermit suddenly appears before her crying, "Rejoice, O mother! Thy son shall be a saint!" Reluctant to speak of this because she fears being accused of pride, she never learns that soon afterwards, as Julian's father is bidding his guests farewell, a gypsy beggar rises up before him muttering, "Ah! Ah! Your son! . . . Much blood! . . . Much glory! . . . Always happy! An emperor's family."

The boy is cherished by his parents, watched over carefully by his three nurses. When he is seven, his mother teaches him to sing and his father delights him by seating him on top of his huge warhorse. His education begins, consisting of lessons from a wise old monk, the stories of passing merchants and pilgrims, and stirring tales told by his father and his old companions-at-arms. But though Julian shouts out at the accounts of siege and battle, he is also pious and charitable. His father is sure he will be a conqueror; his mother convinced he will become an archbishop.

One day in chapel, Julian sees a little white mouse scurry across the floor, and for some reason it fills him with annoyance and hatred. After seeing it again on several Sundays, he shuts himself into the chapel, sprinkles crumbs near the mouse-hole, and waits with a stick. The mouse appears. Julian strikes a slight blow, then stands appalled over the little motionless body. He throws the mouse outside and never speaks of it, but afterwards a kind of rage for killing possesses him. With a blow-pipe he slaughters songbirds in the courtyard and once, wounding a dove, pursues it into the brambles of the moor, to strangle it with a savage delight.

Soon Julian begins his formal lesson in "venery," the art of hunting: how to train dogs and falcons, to set traps, to track the prey, to kill and butcher it. With great packs of dogs of all breeds, he pursues deer, wild boar and bison; rides out with hawks and falcons brought from the Caucasus and Babylon; nets quail; traps wolves and foxes. He prefers, above all, to hunt alone with his white falcon, or to follow his hounds until they bring down the stag and tear it to bits-this delights him. When, in the evening, he returns home covered with blood and mud, he coldly receives the embrace of his mother: his thoughts seem "far away.

Comment

The medieval background is rich and authentic, though created with few words. Especially in his description of hunting, a medieval "specialty," Flaubert evokes the color and savagery of the period. Beauty versus barbarism, piety versus war: in such antitheses we find the key to Flaubert's view of the Middle Ages and to Julian's heredity, upbringing and psychology. The point is not labored, but we can see how the diverse temperaments and ambitions of his parents might create a conflict in Julian and exaggerate his normal boyhood cruelty. Only some sense of guilt could produce that "savage, tumultuous" delight in killing. The idea of the sacrilegiousness of the slaughter of beasts is suggested in Julian's hasty removal of the drop of the mouse's blood with which he has stained the chapel, and his strangling of the dove. We see him, in the end, being estranged from his mother, his gentle side.

One cold winter dawn, Julian sets out with his crossbow and two hounds. First, the dogs kill some rabbits; then, Julian lops off the feet of a sleeping quail, stabs a mountain goat, slaughters lowflying cranes with his whip, shoots a beaver in the middle of a pond. He comes to a sort of "avenue" of tall trees, lined by animals-roebuck, deer, badgers, peacocks, foxes, hedgehogs, lynxes-which move around him trembling, with glances of supplication. But Julian butchers them all, with dreamlike ease and indefatigability. Finally, he sees an amazing sight: a deep valley where stags are packed against each other for warmth. ". . . The certainty of a great slaughter suffocated him with joy." He dismounts and shoots arrow after arrow at the frantic beasts until, under a sky "as red as a sheet of blood," they lie in a dying heap. Julian stares uncomprehendingly at his massacre. Suddenly he sees across the valley an enormous sixteen-point stag with a white beard, accompanied by a hind and her nursing fawn. "Once more the bow twanged." The fawn falls dead and the mother raises her head in a cry of human lamentation, to be killed herself a moment later. The huge stag leaps toward Julian, who shoots his last arrow. It lodges in the stag's forehead, but

MADAME BOVARY AND THREE TALES

he does not seems to feel it. Julian retreats in terror, but the stag stops short and cries in a terrible voice, "Accursed! Accursed! One day, O vicious heart, thou shalt murder thy father and mother!"

Weary and heartsick, he finds his way back to the castle. Obsessed by the stag's words, he cannot sleep that night. He could not kill his parents, he tells himself, but suppose he wanted to . . . if the devil made him want to . . .? For three months afterwards he is sick, and when he recovers he refuses to hunt. One day, climbing a ladder to get a heavy sword, Julian drops the weapon and it cuts his father's robe. Thinking he has killed him, Julian faints. Thereafter, he will not touch a weapon until his family begs him, in the name of his honor and ancestors, to resume the "exercises of a gentlemen." Practicing with a javelin in the courtyard one day, Julian sees what he takes to be the fluttering wings of a stork behind a tree, and launches his weapon. He hears his mother scream: it is her white bonnet which he has pinned to the wall. Julian flees the castle, never to return.

Comment

The account of Julian's hunt is an amazing combination of reality and dream: his natural prowess and bloodthirstiness, the natural abundance of wild-life, melting into supernaturally unerring and tireless slaughter amidst a flood of beast. Supernatural stags are common in medieval legend, and frequently symbolize Christ. The white beard of Julian's stag suggests, however, the beard of his father. We come now to the deeper meanings of Julian's love of hunting: it is a substitute for parricide, perhaps even a form of vicarious self-murder. Julian clearly recognizes in his own heart the possibility of a desire to kill his mother and father, and perhaps his "accidents" are more like attempts.

SECTION TWO

Julian joins a band of adventurers and soon, through his strength, bravery and skill, becomes captain of a company. He comes to know the hardships of campaigns, the terrors of battle and assault, but always "Divine favor" spares his life. He protects churchmen, orphans, widows, and the old especially. Whenever he sees an old man he makes him show his face, as if he were afraid of killing him. He becomes famous, helping the Kings of France and England in battle, traveling to remote corners of the world to deliver oppressed peoples and imprisoned queens, righting wrongs and slaying monsters. Finally, he frees the Emperor of Occitania from the captivity of the Caliph of Cordova. Julian refuses all the rewards offered him, until the Emperor brings forth his daughter. The moment he sees the black-eyed, slender girl, Julian falls in love with her, and soon they are married.

With the daughter of the Emperor Julian lives in a white marble palace in Moorish style, among gardens and orange trees overlooking a bay. Within, the rooms are exquisitely decorated and filled with "sweet silence." Julian makes war no longer, but sometimes in the midst of his peaceful people, he recalls his hunts of former days or dreams at night that the animals are parading before him as before Adam in Paradise or Noah, and he kills them all with a motion of his arm. Still, he refuses to hunt, thinking that the fate of his parents depends on this. But the longing grows unbearable. He tells his wife on his obsession, and she argues that his parents must be dead by now; anyway, why should he kill them? He cannot be persuaded.

MADAME BOVARY AND THREE TALES

Comment

Julian's solution is merely another form of killing. Though disguised by the chivalric code, as the brutality of hunting is disguised by the formal code of venery, warfare is murder. Julian cannot evade his bloodthirsty human nature or his destiny. His life with the Emperor's daughter is too dreamlike and inactive to satisfy him and his "subconscious" compensates with dreams of universal slaughter.

One evening, Julian hears the yelping of a fox and soft footsteps outside his chamber. He cannot, at last, resist going out, though his wife now has dark forebodings. Soon after Julian has left, a page introduces an old man and woman. They are Julian's father and mother, who have spent years searching for their son. All their money has gone and they have been reduced to rags and beggary, but they are delighted by Julian's good fortune and his lovely wife and look forward rapturously to embracing their son. Their daughter-in-law puts them to bed in her own chamber.

Meanwhile Julian walks into the moonlit forest. It is filled with deep silence, warm enervating airs and odors. A boar leaps out behind him, too quickly for Julian to shoot. He spies a wolf, and the animal lures him deeper into the wilderness by always running out of bowshot. At last he comes to a stony plateau littered with corpses, bones and crypts among which hyenas prowl. They grin at him and run off when he unsheathes his sword. An hour later, he meets a wild bull. He spears it, but his lance breaks "as if the animal were made of bronze." He closes his eyes, expecting death, but the bull disappears. Julian is in an agony of shame: some "superior power" is destroying his strength. He turns to go home, stumbling over vines while animals continually cross his path. He sees "a galaxy of sparks" among the branches: the eyes of wildcats, monkeys, owls, squirrels . . . Julian shoots arrow after arrow: all miss. He throws stones: all fall short. Choking with rage, he screams imprecations at them.

All the animals he has ever killed gather in a circle around him. Terrified, Julian begins to walk slowly toward the castle, escorted by the beasts. All their movements seem "ironical." They brush up against him, beat him with their wings, suffocate him with their breath. A panther disdainfully drops an arrow at his foot. Suddenly a cock crows. The animals disappear and Julian recognizes the roof of his palace. At the edge of the field he sees some partridges in the stubble and drops his cloak over them. When he lifts it, he finds one bird, long dead and decaying.

This "mockery" renews his thirst for killing: "for want of beasts he longed to slaughter men." He thinks, though, that his wife may calm his spirit, and goes to her room. In the dim light he bends over to kiss her, and feels a beard against his lips. He draws back, reaches out again. "A man! A man in bed with his wife!" In uncontrollable fury he strikes out with his dagger, "stamping and fuming" like "a beast gone mad." Then, mingling with the low death rattles of his victim, he hears in the distance, growing louder, the braying of the great stag.

Julian's wife stands in the doorway with a torch. Immediately she understands what has happened and flees in horror. Julian picks up her torch and looks down upon the faces of his mother and father, which "majestic in their gentleness, seemed to be guarding an eternal secret."

The room is spattered with blood and a red light pours in through the stained glass windows.

At the end of the day, Julian comes to his wife to tell her he must renounce everything and never see her again. Three days later, his parents are buried with great ceremony in a monastery chapel. The procession is followed by a man in monk's habit, to whom no one dares speak. During the mass he remains outside the chapel stretched cross-wise in the dust. Afterwards, he is seen taking the road that disappears among the mountains.

Comment

The second hunt reverses that of Section One. It is night, rather than morning, and instead of winter's cold there is warmth and the odor of decay. Rather than Julian being irresistible, the animals are invulnerable; rather than dying, they are resurrected; rather than Julian being the hunter, he is their victim. Across a nightmare landscape which suggests the carnage of Julian's military career, the beasts escort him to his destiny. They mock him because they know that he, a man, is more helplessly the victim of his thirst for blood, than they were of his spear or arrow, and that once man has drawn the sword, inevitably he will plunge it into the bodies most dearly loved, the very sources of his being. The animals, too, are mostly savage and repulsive: hyenas, serpents, wolves, panthers, suggesting that it is the lusts and evil passions of Julian's nature, which he cannot slay and never thought of slaying, that lead him to his crime.

The transformation of Julian's thirst for killing beasts into a thirst for human victims is typical of his life. His bestial behavior during the killing hints at a further **irony**: who is more a beast, an animal or a man killing? We feel that the murder is less inspired by Julian's jealousy or sense of honor, than by his vicious and "animal" nature's need to kill. If it had not been his parents, not been "jealousy," he would have found some other victim, some other pretext.

SECTION THREE

Julians becomes a beggar along the highways. His face is so sad that no one refuses him alms, but when he tells his story all shrink from him in horror. Those who recognize him shut the doors against him and shout abuse. Usually he avoids the company of men, living in the wilderness on roots and wild fruits, but occasionally he is drawn into towns by "the need to mingle with the life of others." The people's looks of cruelty and distraction disturb him, but worse is the sight on feast days of families at table, the grandparents with their grandchildren on their knees. Then, sobbing bitterly, he returns to the country.

He gazes at the young animals with love, but they all run from him in terror. In dreams he nightly reenacts the murder of his parents. Though he mortifies his flesh and repeatedly risks his life rescuing people from fires and ravines, he finds no peace. He resolves to die, but one day, glancing into a spring, he sees the face of an old man with a white beard and "a look so piteous that it was impossible for him to hold back his tears." The face is so like his father's that Julian gives up the idea of killing himself.

At length, after many years of wandering, he comes to an impassable slime-banked river in a northern land. He sees an old boat half-buried in the mud and decides to serve others by becoming a ferry-man. With great labor he constructs a stone pier into the river, then builds himself a rude hut. Travelers begin to come, paying him with left-over food and worn-out clothing, or curses and blasphemies. Julian blesses all. The countryside is a barren plain, spotted with "ghostly ponds": a land which in spring gives forth the odor of decay. There are violent winds and clouds of mosquitoes, and a long winter of terrible cold. For months Julian sees no one: his only company is the memories of his childhood, interrupted by frightful visions of his crime.

One night he is awakened by a calling voice. Rising, he hears only the wind, but the voice repeats, "Julian!" He crosses the stormy waters to find a hideous Leper with burning eyes and a strange "kingly majesty" in his posture. The Leper enters the boat, which sinks low under his weight, and with infinite labor, "knowing that this passage was of great importance," Julian rows him across.

The Leper enters his hut. His rags fall from him revealing a gruesomely scarred and ulcerated body. His nose has been eaten away and his breath is nauseous. "I am hungry!" he says. Julian gives him his food, noticing, when the meal is finished that the table, cutlery, etc., are now splotched like the stranger's body. "I am thirsty!" Julian brings his pitcher which gives forth a delicious odor of wine. The Leper drinks it all, then says, "I am cold!" Julian makes a fire, but the Leper still trembles and demands, "Thy bed!" Julian wraps him up carefully, but then the Leper commands him to strip and lie beside him that he may have the warmth of Julian's body.

Julian lies beside the stranger, feeling his cold rough body against him. Panting, the Leper orders him to move closer and warm him, not with his hands only but with his whole body. "Julian stretched himself out, mouth to mouth, breast to breast." Then the Leper embraces him and his eyes suddenly sparkle like stars, his breath was the fragrance of roses, incense rises from the hearth and the waves sing. While Julian's heart is flooded with delight, the Leper grows until his arms and feet touch the walls of the hut. "Then the roof flew off, the firmament opened -

and Julian ascended toward the blue expanses, face to face with Our Lord Jesus, who bore him to Heaven."

Comment

Fundamental to the *Legend of St. Julian* is the idea that his salvation comes as much through humble service as through self-mortification. In fact, it is only after he has set up his ferry service, that God provides the occasion for a saving act of self-mortification: the embrace of the Leper. The simplest interpretation of this act is that it shows a perfected charity which extends itself to any object, however repulsive. It is a simultaneous act of self-mortification and love, in which each validates the other.

But other complications are involved in Flaubert's version of St. Julian. Especially, we note the recurrent idea of corruption in the last part of the tale: in the hunt, the landscape of Julian's retreat, the body of the Leper. Julian's salvation seems to depend upon his willingness to accept, even "embrace" this corruption. It is as if all his bloodthirstiness has been a retaliation upon the world for some inward sense of guilt or decay, which he must acknowledge to find peace. The Leper, moreover, is not simply "Our Lord Jesus," but can be identified with both Julian himself and his father: as an embodiment of the inner corruption of the former, as the latter returning from the grave to at last embrace his lost son, his murderer.

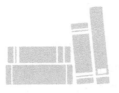

THREE TALES

HERODIAS

. . . .

SECTION ONE

The scene of *Herodias* is the citadel of Machaerus, stronghold of the Tetrarch Herod Antipas, ruler of Palestine under the Roman protectorate. It is dawn, and Antipas is staring out over the battlements at the arid landscape below him, jagged and deeply shadowed in the morning light. In the distance he sees the camp of the King of Arabs, whose daughter he divorced to marry Herodias, the wife of his own brother, Agrippa. Antipas is awaiting help from the Roman governor of Syria, Vitellius, but in the meantime is considering a number of other plans and alliances. His meditations are broken by a faint, subterranean cry, and he hastily summons Mannaeus the executioner, his faithful servant. Mannaeus assures him that the dungeon still safely holds the man Iaokanann, whom the Latins call St. John the Baptist.

While Mannaeus stands on the parapet cursing the Temple of Jerusalem visible among the far off hills-as a Samaritan, he hates the Jews - Herodias appears. She is carelessly dressed, having just come from her chamber with the good news that her ex-husband, Antipas' brother Agrippa, has been imprisoned by the Emperor Tiberius. Herodias boasts of the role she has played in eliminating this potential menace, reminds Antipas of her many sacrifices for him (including the abandonment of her daughter Salome), and recalls to him the days of their early love in Italy. But that was twelve years ago: Antipas blames her for all his troubles and no longer cares for her.

An Essene (one of a particularly pious and ascetic Jewish sect) named Phanuel arrives. He has come to beg the Tetrarch to release Iaokanann. Antipas feels, however, that Iaokanann may prove to be a useful hostage, while Herodias, who has been insulted and cursed by the prophet as an adulteress, wishes to have him killed. She commences a long tirade, touching upon Iaokanann, Antipas' deficiency as a ruler, the baseness of his ancestry, his lechery. Meanwhile, her husband, gazing down on the valley, is struck by the beauty of a young girl half-concealed by the shade of a parasol, who appears on one of the rooftops. He asks Herodias who she is, but his wife, with an air of satisfaction, says she has no idea, and leaves.

Phanuel resumes his appeal for the delivery of Iaokanann. "In spite of myself, I love him," says that Tetrarch, but the prophet has followers and is his enemy. He remembers that Phanuel had some other important news for him, but, before the Essene can answer him, a messenger interrupts with word of the arrival of the Proconsul Vitellius. A rush of preparation ensues.

Comment

The atmosphere and background of ancient Palestine are achieved almost entirely without recourse to extended description or **exposition**. The central figure is Antipas, a man remarkable for his self-division and distraction of mind: "... the Tetrarch was weary of reflection ... Antipas seemed lost in a vision . . .," etc. Over and over, he is not paying attention to the subject at hand, or thinking two things at once, or dropping one puzzle to take up another, or balancing one consideration against half a dozen others. Only two things seem to arouse a strong response: the cry of Iaokanann from the pit, and the sight of the girl on the rooftop.

SECTION TWO

Vitellius enters surrounded by his ceremonial guard and followed by a heavy red litter. The litter carries his son Aulus, a fat, pimply-faced glutton cherished by his father since the latter's eminence stems from Aulus' perverted relationship with the emperor Tiberius. The Tetrarch and Proconsul exchange formal compliments under which runs a vein of suspicion and dislike. In the midst of their greetings, Vitellius' soldiers begin to arrive and a mob of Sadducees and Pharisees (Jewish sects traditionally associated with an exaggerated and hypocritical piety). There is a turmoil of presentations, suits, denunciations, made to both Tetrarch and Proconsul. Antipas explains that so many people are present because it is his birthday, and points to enormous baskets of food being raised into the citadel. The excited glutton Aulus insists on an immediate visit to the kitchens.

A tour of the citadel follows, Antipas uneasily conducting the Romans through the underground chambers filled with armaments, and into his subterranean stable where marvelous white horses inflame the Romans' cupidity. Finally, they come to a courtyard where Vitellius notices that one of the bronze shields set into the pavement rings hollow. Thinking that it conceals the treasure of Herod, Vitellius demands that the shield be lifted. Antipas complies.

Far down below, they see a strange figure with long hair, wearing a hair shirt. It is Iaokanann, John the Baptist. First a sigh rises out of the pit, then terrifying vituperation against the Sadducees and Pharisees which modulates to prophesy of the golden age coming with the dominion of the "Son of David." Spying Antipas and Herodias, Iaokanann renews his invective: the Tetrarch, for his adultery, has been afflicted with "the sterility of a mule," while his wife is a "Jezebel," who will "die like a dog." The trapdoor is lowered again.

While a debate rages on the question of the legitimacy of Antipas' marriage to Herodias, Aulus returns and assures the Tetrarch that it is ridiculous to be disturbed by the Jewish taboos. When Herodias declares that Iaokanann has been urging the people to refuse to pay taxes, all the Romans approve of his imprisonment and Vitellius stations guards around the dungeon. Antipas is relieved to have the matter taken out of his hands. He tells Phanuel that there is now nothing he can do for Iaokanann. The Essene then discloses to the Tetrarch that his reading of the stars has shown that an important man is to die in Machaerus that night. Disturbed, Antipas goes to his wife's chambers, to see there, for one moment, a woman's arm of surpassing beauty emerge from behind a curtain. Herodias does not identify the woman.

Comment

The crucial scene in this section is the disclosure of Iaokanann in his pit. In the midst of all the confusion, cross-purpose, bickering, and corruption, his is a clear voice, as if the voice of

Antipas' buried conscience. But even Iaokanann's voice is not absolutely clear. His prophesies of the golden age are naive and will be unfulfilled, his denunciations are ineffectual and perhaps oversimplified, and he himself is not completely certain of his role. Though he repeats to himself, "That He may increase, I must decrease!" he does not yet fully accept or understand his fate.

SECTION THREE

The enormous banquet hall is filled. Candles blaze off the cups and copper dishes, slaves wearing felt slippers hurry among the guests. Antipas, Vitellius and Aulus recline, Roman-style, on ivory couches at the head of the hall. All are elaborately dressed. Aulus is attended by a pretty little boy he has found in the kitchens.

A debate breaks out among the Jewish guests about Iaokanann and other prophets and healers. Jesus is mentioned and one of the guests swears he has witnessed one of his miracles. He claims that Jesus is the Messiah. The discussion turns to that peculiar Jewish belief: the Messiah must be a son of David, not of a carpenter; he must confirm the Law, not attack it; besides, he is to be heralded by Elias . . . "But Elias has come," insists the man, his name is "Iaokanann!"

While Aulus is vomiting to prepare himself for a new bout of gluttony, the discussion shifts to immortality and the resurrection. The Proconsul's son recovers and throws himself on new dishes: honeyed gourds, nightingales, dormice, bull kidneys. The guests, Jews, Asiatics, Greeks, Northerners, talk about their native gods. The order of the feast is disturbed by cries from the ravine below the citadel of a mob demanding the release of Iaokanann, and by a sudden outbreak among the

Pharisees, who discover that they have been served a stew of wild ass, an unclean meat.

The banquet approaches its conclusion. Vitellius broods darkly on the intolerance and unruliness of the Jews, overhearing them talk rebellion at a nearby table-while Antipas trembles. Aulus lies in a stupor: "too full to indulge himself more, but too obstinate to leave." Suddenly Herodias appears, followed by a figure that causes the crowd to gasp with admiration. It is a young girl, half-hidden by a long bluish veil and dressed in ornate, bejeweled clothing. When she throws back her veil, she seems like Herodias young again: it is her daughter Salome.

The girl begins to dance to the music of flutes and castanets. Her movements are exquisite, incredibly sensual, and all the rapt men are filled with "fiery longing." She dances toward Antipas, who, sobbing with desire, calls to her to come to him, promising her castles, cities, provinces, anything. She stops. In a lisping girlish voice, she says "I want you to give me on a platter the head . . . of Iaokanann." Herodias has trained her well, to make sure of Antipas.

The Tetrarch recoils in horror, but he has given his word. Besides, perhaps Iaokanann's is the eminent death foretold by Phanuel, and if he is really Elias he cannot be killed anyway. Mannaeus the executioner is sent to the dungeon, but returns after a while greatly upset. He has seen the "Great Angel of the Samaritans" guarding the pit with a flaming sword. All, and especially Herodias, upbraid him furiously and the shamed executioner leaves again. After a long wait, he reenters the banquet hall holding at arm's length by its hair the head of Iaokanann. The head is presented to Salome, then circulated among the guests. It rests for a moment before the waking Aulus, who stares at it with dull eyes, and finally comes to a stop before the weeping Antipas. Long after all the guests have left, the Tetrarch sits at the table gazing at the severed head, while Phanuel mumbles prayers with arms outstretched.

In the morning the two men sent out long ago by Iaokanann deliver a message to Phanuel which leaves the Essene "enraptured." Presumably, Jesus has declared that Iaokanann is indeed Elias, the forerunner, and that his death has been divinely ordained. Phanuel points to the bloody head amidst the remnants of the feast, and one of the messengers says, "Be consoled! He has gone down to the dead to announce the Christ!" Phanuel now understands Iaokanann's words: "I must decrease, that He may increase." The three men carry away the head in the direction of Galilee.

Comment

The most significant fact, perhaps, is that Antipas, after seeing the head of Iaokanann, shows no interest in enjoying his dreadful bargain. He seems to have forgotten Salome. The martyrdom of Iaokanann is received with perfect indifference by all the guests, but the Tetrarch alone has an inkling of what it means. Antipas is a man whose character or fate will not allow him to be one thing or the other, neither the believer nor the unmitigated sensualist. He is too complicated, too "modern," and therefore "sterile," thus the ideal witness (for Flaubert) of the great events ushering in the Christian era. What we forget and what Herodias emphasizes is that these were, in fact, not "great" events to the general consciousness of the time, nor were such figures as John the Baptist haloed and unmistakable Hollywood saints, but men of ordinary, if not eccentric appearance. Thus, the martyrdom of a saint is merely a grotesque after-dinner diversion to men in their ordinary distractions and brutishness.

THREE TALES

CRITICAL COMMENTARY

The *Three Tales* were written in 1870, during a prolonged vacation which Flaubert was allowing himself from the agonies involved in the writing of his last novel, *Bouvard and Pecuchet*. It was the most enthusiastically received of all Flaubert's works, and shows him at the mature height of his powers. Two of the Tales, *A Simple Heart* and *The Legend of St. Julian the Hospitaller*, are unquestionably masterpieces of short fiction.

THEIR SIGNIFICANCE

Many critics have remarked on the way the *Three Tales* epitomizes the three main strands of Flaubert's life work. In its contemporary **realism**, *A Simple Heart* is akin to *Madame Bovary*, the *Sentimental Education* and *Bouvard and Pecuchet*. Felicite, in fact, seems to be a development of the old domestic, Catherine Ledoux, of the first novel. The visionary St. Julian is related to his earlier fragment of a saint's life, the *Temptation of St. Anthony*. The exotic *Herodias* is the "sister" to *Salammbo*, his Carthaginian romance. Flaubert, indeed, intended each of the Tales to be representative of one of the three major phases of Western history, as he conceived it: "paganisme," "Christianisme," and "muflisme" - the last, the modern era, can be translated as "brutism" or "boorism." His earlier novels had also been concerned with these three periods.

THEIR STYLES

Each tale has distinct and appropriate stylistic qualities. *A Simple Heart* is a masterpiece of subtly evocative **realism**. It is written in Flaubert's barest, most disciplined style, in a manner suitable to the deprived and self-denying life it depicts. *St. Julian*, on the other hand, has all the freshness and color, the vitality and sharpness of contrast of medieval life and art. Its qualities are reminiscent of a stained-glass window, such as the window in the Rouen Cathedral which inspired Flaubert to write the story. The style of *Herodias* is colorful and exotic, too, but designedly lacks the vivacity and charm of *St. Julian*. Where one is a vision, the other is a trance: there is something unhealthy and oppressive about its atmosphere, a sense of theatrical hollowness and artificiality.

THEIR SIMILARITIES

Despite their stylistic differences, the three stories have many underlying similarities. At the center of each is a "saint" and "martyrdom": the servant Felicite, Julian, Iaokanann or St. John the Baptist. Each reveals Flaubert's fascination for the mystic or visionary, his admiration for a life of dedicated labor and self-sacrifice. In each case, too, the sanctity of the **protagonist** is curiously shadowed and ambiguous. We are never sure whether it is the Holy Ghost coming to Felicite in the form of a parrot, or whether it is merely the pathetic delusion of a simple-minded old woman. Julian's story, too, is far from being Flaubert's personal assertion of his sainthood. The actuality of Julian's sainthood is qualified by the fantastic quality of the tale, and by Flaubert's disavowal of responsibility in the final line: "And that is the story of St. Julian the Hospitaller, more or less as it is found on the stained-glass windows of a church in my own province." He is saying, in other words, "It is not my story." Moreover, in Julian's whole career and especially in the final embrace of the Leper, there are a multitude of dark and unsaintly implications. Finally, Iaokanann is presented in Herodias as a rather vague and bizarre figure, whose credentials for sainthood are not yet fully established. Besides, the central figure in the last tale is not the prophet, but the Tetrarch, Herod Antiphas.

THE MAIN CHARACTERS

The three principal characters of the *Tales* present a number of interesting contrasts. Though, ostensibly, *A Simple Heart* is the "modern" tale, *St. Julian* the medieval tale, and *Herodias* the ancient, these categories are somewhat misleading. While Julian is clearly a medieval figure, Felicite is really of no particular time at all; she is the kind of simple, unhistorical creature that has existed in almost every age. And Antipas, though nominally the most ancient figure, is in most respects essentially a "modern" man, with all his complexity, chronic self-division and anxiety, his vacillation between the possibility of faith and the pursuit of power and sensual gratification. The three characters also represent, perhaps, three different possibilities relative to sainthood. Felicite is the unified saint, one who moves with her whole being along a clear and straight road to sanctity. Julian's path to sainthood is by way of the most violent self-conflict and unspeakable crime. Antipas is the representative modern man, one who cannot commit himself fully enough to any side of his nature to become either saint or sinner. As Felicite is a "martyr" to bourgeois callousness and exploitation, as Julian is to Destiny or Providence and his own character, so Antipas suffers "martyrdom" from an historical situation which does not allow him a full heart for anything.

ESSAY QUESTIONS AND ANSWERS

Question: What are the resemblances between Felicite's life in *A Simple Heart* and the conventional life of a saint?

Answer: There are a number of kinds of evidence conventionally cited in proof of saintliness: (1) The individual's life conforms outwardly to the practices and doctrines of the Church. (2) The individual engages in a struggle against pride, self-interest and attachment to achieve perfect humility and disinterested charity. (3) His life shows evidence of Providential intervention at crucial moments. (4) His election is indicated by miracles, special suffering or martyrdom.

Felicite's life satisfies these requirements, but not unambiguously. (1) Within the limits of her understanding, she is a good Catholic, following the ordinances of her faith. Her confusion of the parrot with the Holy Ghost is not necessarily heresy: the Lamb and the Dove are themselves only symbols. But perhaps Felicite gives the symbol too much independent life, and converting it into an object of idolatry, ends by worshipping the parrot, not the reality behind it. (2) Felicite does have moments when she resents the callousness of her employer, but typically forgives her and returns to her work. Her successive attachments may seem thoroughly unselfish, especially her love for the parrot from whom she can get nothing but the mere joy of loving him. But Loulou does remain a material possession, something of hers which she dotes on. Her love for him may be the reverse of saintly nonattachment and love of God: absurd dotage on a petty, decaying object. (3) Perhaps the hand of Providence is visible in the losses of Felicite's life, which wean her away from the world. However, if we cannot otherwise establish that she is a saint, such losses, which are common, cannot be proven Providential. (4) Felicite's "mystical" experiences are highly ambiguous. Her communion with Loulou and her climactic dying vision may be naive, but genuine religious experiences, or blasphemous absurdities. (5) Felicite's early "miracles" are only miraculous in that they parallel famous saintly encounters with savage beasts, not as involving any suspension of natural law. Her life has much suffering and her experience on the road to Honfleur resembles the scourging of Christ before the crucifixion. If she endures a martyrdom, it is of a gradual, life-long kind, and perhaps her fortitude and gentleness in bearing it are as remarkable as serenity under physical torture.

Question: Other than "Destiny" or "Providence," what are the determinants of Julian's strange career in *The Legend of St. Julian the Hospitaller*?

Answer: Julian's tragedy arises from the nature of medieval civilization, the special circumstances of his upbringing, and the general nature of man. Flaubert evidently conceives of the Middle Ages as combining many diametrically opposed qualities: refinement and brutality, gentleness and cruelty, piety and lawlessness, etc. As a representative medieval man, Julian embodies these qualities. Moreover, their conflict in him is heightened by the opposition of his parents: his gentle, pious mother who dreams of her son becoming a saint, his old warrior father who dreams of conquest. The saint and the soldier are the two opposing ideal men of the Middle Ages.

Seemingly, the masculine, warrior side of Julian wins out at first, but in an exaggerated and morbid form. His bloodthirstiness suggests not only that he is playing a role to the hilt, but compensating for some inhibited drive or venting on substitutes a murderous impulse toward other, forbidden objects. Clearly, it is his parents he really wants to kill, possibly out of some complicated Oedipal-homosexual relationship to them, but perhaps more because they embody the principles so bitterly conflicting in him. Moreover since these principles are in himself as well as in his parents, his impulse is not only parricidal, but suicidal. The gentle, supplicating animals he slaughters so mercilessly in his first hunt suggest his feminine, saintly side which he tries to "kill."

When Julian's masculine prowess achieves the ultimate reward, recognition as a hero and the gift of an Emperor's daughter, he finds the reward hollow. He is not really happy at receiving what one gets for successfully "being a man" in the narrow, secular sense. His old conflicts emerge, and finally he cannot be satisfied by mere dreams of universal slaughter, he needs actual blood. The second hunt discloses, first, that Julian's whole career-a long succession of murders-is futile and rotten: the corpses of his victims litter the plateau and the dead beasts return to life. Moreover, he finds himself strangely "impotent" or "feminized": such are the inescapable Freudian implications of his breaking his lance against the bull, or the panther dropping the arrow at his feet. Under the circumstances, one can see how the sight of his wife in bed with another man would be particularly horrifying: it would seem an ultimate mockery of his new condition. At this point, too, his hatred of his parents would reach the highest intensity: they are the causes of his agony.

Julian's penance involves the renunciation of his former character, an assumption of the role and values his mother had stood for. His embrace of the Leper seems, therefore, not only a gesture of penance and charity, but a final coming to terms with the side of his nature he has always suppressed and corrupted, or with the inevitable human corruption which he has always been afraid to face. The contemporary reader, especially in view of what has gone before, cannot fail to find homosexual implications in the embrace. But it is probably truer to the intention of the story to say that, in embracing the most horrible of human conditions (leprosy), Julian is at last accepting and forgiving himself for his own human corruption. With this self-acceptance, self-forgiveness, comes the acceptance of Christ, who was also able to "embrace" human corruption.

Question: What is the relationship between Antipas and Iaokanann and its bearing upon the general **theme** of *Herodias?*

Answer: From the beginning of the story we see that the relationship between Antipas and Iaokanann is a strange one. First, the prophet's imprisonment seems to have been the idea of *Herodias,* Antipas' evil side. ("Evil" in that she is closest to the schemer and lecher in him.) The Tetrarch confesses that he "loves" Iaokanann, but is terrified of his escape or of anyone learning he has such a captive. The man is "dangerous" to him. On the other side, the prophet's denunciations of Herodias are much stronger than his attacks on the Tetrarch. He even speaks as if the incest-adultery of their marriage was all Herodias' fault: she seduced Antipas with "the creaking of her slipper." The closeness of the two men is suggested by Antipas' peculiar sensitivity to Iaokanann. He is able to hear the latter's voice through the "bowels of the earth."

Iaokanann may represent, then, a part of himself Antipas has suppressed or "buried": less his conscience, perhaps, than a capacity for faith or commitment. This suppression has been made for what a highly civilized man like Antipas would deem "good reason." For Iaokanann, whatever his holiness and moral superiority, seems a strange wild creature, fanatical and even a bit cracked. Similarly, Antipas' relationship to the sensual (as opposed to the spiritual) is also half-hearted. Though he madly desires Salome for a moment, he pays no attention to her after their bargain; and since she is only "Herodias grown young again," his ultimate disenchantment with her would be inevitable. Sensuality, however, is "on top": out in the sunlight, on the rooftops and battlements, while faith is buried in the pit. In the Tetrarch's world, sensuality, gluttony, greed, or ambitions are more respectable than faith.

We are not made privy to Antipas' thoughts as he gazes at Iaokanann's head among the debris of the banquet, but he must have a sense of desolating loss and failure. At the bidding of passion and policy he has eliminated a major alternative of his nature. During such a time as that of Antipas, and with such a character as his-complicated, self-divided, sceptical-the miracles and opportunity of faith will be dubious and neglected. Yet, afterwards, he will have an inkling of the extent of his self-betrayal. Through his hero, Flaubert is showing how doubtful and shadowy the most significant events are when isolated from their historical consequences, and how ill-equipped are most contemporary men to respond adequately to them. To most of the men living in their day, John and Jesus must have seemed questionable or deluded characters, even admitting "something remarkable" about them.

THREE TALES

· ·

SUMMARY OF CRITICISM

The critical judgements of and approaches to *Madame Bovary* have been enormously varied. Much of the best writing on the book, naturally, is in French, but the following will give the student some idea of the positions and interests of a number of important critics.

Two of the earliest pieces on *Madame Bovary* are reviews by Sainte-Beuve and Baudelaire. Sainte-Beuve rather stuffily commends the book's excellence of style, but deplores the fact that there is not a single good character in it. The book is cruel and an unfair representation of provincial life. Baudelaire, on the other hand, in enthusiastic: Flaubert has deliberately chosen the most vulgar and overworked subject, adultery, the most stupid of all backgrounds, the provinces, and transmuted them by supreme artistry. Emma may not be morally good, but she is "sublime," a noble fusion of masculine and feminine qualities.

Subsequent criticism, up to the modern day, seems to have followed these alternatives: praise of the art, and condemnation of Flaubert's negativism. Andre Gide, while being deeply attached to Flaubert's work, found him guilty of the "blasphemy of life," while Mauriac accused him of eliminating the soul from human beings in order to obtain "stupidity in the pure state." Such writers as Proust and Sartre show a similar ambivalence. The tendency of the most recent criticism seems to be more favorable to Flaubert and exhibits a greater concern for questions of technique and style. It is typical of more recent critics, too, to show a keener interest in *Sentimental Education* and *Bouvard and Pecuchet*, which have been less popular works.

COMMENT ON BIBLIOGRAPHY

Students who wish to explore Flaubert criticism in preparation for papers or examinations may find the following survey of the Bibliography useful.

The books by Alison Fairlie and M. G. Tillett are good general discussions of the meaning and style of *Madame Bovary*, of particular value as introductions to the major problems of the novel. Raymond Giraud, Harry Levin and Martin Turnell have written interesting analyses of Flaubert's mind and art. The first is especially valuable for his discussion of the cultural and literary background of Flaubert's work, while Levin is more concerned with the artist's psychology and its reflection in his style. Turnell, who feels that Flaubert was "a great writer with whom there was something badly wrong," has helpful comments on *Madame Bovary.*

Eric Auerbach's book has a suggestive chapter on some of the innovations and qualities of style in *Madame Bovary*, a matter which is taken up at length in Anthony Thorlby's somewhat difficult and philosophical study of Flaubert's **realism**. Stylistic questions are also the major concern of Hugh Kenner's book and Benjamin Bart's analysis of Flaubert's use of landscape description. Flaubert's relationship to politics and society is a basic issue with Jean-Paul Sartre and Edmund Wilson, though Sartre also deals with the psychological question of why Flaubert, In *Madame Bovary*, "metamorphosed himself into a woman." Both critics are Marxians, but while Sartre accuses Flaubert of showing bad faith to the working class when he was so alienated from the bourgeoisie, Wilson is concerned to show the undercurrents of social thought in Flaubert's work. Georges Poulet, finally, considers the effects of Flaubert's habits of perception and memory, his semi-mystical experiences, on his writing. *Selections from Poulet,* Levin, Turnell, Auerbach, Sartre, and a number of other recent critics are found in *Twentieth Century Views*, edited by Giraud.

Among critical biographies of Flaubert, Albert Thibaudet's is the definitive work, but Francis Steegmuller's book is particularly concerned with the experiences that contributed to the writing of *Madame Bovary*. Flaubert's letters are fascinating and revealing, prized by Andre Gide above the novels.

BIBLIOGRAPHY

Auerbach, Eric. *Mimeses.* Princeton: Princeton University Press, 1953

Bart, Benjamin F. *Flaubert's Landscape Description.* Ann Arbor: University of Michigan Press, 1957

Fairlie, Alison. *Flaubert: Madame Bovary.* London: Edward Arnold, 1962

Giraud, Raymond. ed. *Flaubert: Twentieth Century Views.* Englewood Cliffs, N. J.: Prentice-Hall. 1964

The Unheroic Hero in the Novels of Stendhal, Balzac and Flaubert. New Brunswick, N. J.: Rutgers University Press, 1956

James, Henry. *Future of the novel.* New York: Alfred Knopf (Vintage Books), 1959

Kenner, Hugh. Flaubert, Joyce, *Becket: The Stoic Comedians.* Boston: Beacon Press, 1962

Lapp, John C. *Art and Hallucination in Flaubert.* French Studies, X (1956), 322-344

Levin, Harry. *The Gates of Horn.* New York: Oxford University Press, 1963

Poulet, Georges. *Studies in Human Time.* Baltimore: Johns Hopkins Press, 1956

Sartre, John Paul. *Search for a Method.* New York: Alfred A. Knopf, 1963

Steegmuller, Francis (ed. and tr.) *Sainte-Beuve: Selected Essays,* New York: Doubleday and Co., 1963

Thorlby, Anthony. *Gustave Flaubert and the Art of **Realism**.* London: Bowes and Bowes, 1956

Thibaudet, Albert. *Gustave Flaubert.* Paris: Gallimard, 1935

Tillett, M. G. *On Reading Flaubert.* London: Oxford University Press, 1961

Turnell, Martin. *Madame Bovary. The Sewanee Review,* LXV, 4 (October-December, 1957), 531-550

The Novel in France. New York: New Directions, 1951

Wilson, Edmund. *The Triple Thinkers.* New York: Charles Scribners Sons, 1938

BIOGRAPHY AND CORRESPONDENCE

Shanks, Lewis Piaget. *Flaubert's Youth: 1821-1845.* Baltimore: Johns Hopkins Press, 1927

Spencer, Philip. *Flaubert: A Biography.* New York: Grove Press, 1953

Steegmuller, Francis. *Flaubert and Madame Bovary: A Double Portrait.* New York: Farrar, Strauss & Young, 1951.

(tr. and ed.) *Selected Letters of Gustave Flaubert.* New York: Farrar, Strauss & Cudahy, 1954

Lightning Source UK Ltd.
Milton Keynes UK
UKHW020054191220
375492UK00008B/246